A SUMMER
in
IRELAND

Life and Golf on the Emerald Isle

TABA DALE

CLARE HOUSE PUBLISHING

ISBN 978-0-9855193-1-5

First Edition.

Front cover: Liscannor Castle Ruin, County Clare
Back cover (inset): Lahinch Castle Course, 7th Hole, Double Rainbow
Photography by Taba Dale

For, and with Kevin

ACKNOWLEDGEMENTS

Thanks go to Steve Goscin, who is the first person to put it into my head that I should create a book. If it were not for his encouragement, this collection of stories would be nothing more than a hodge-podge, going out into the Universe one-by-one.

To Cliff Carle, my editor extraordinaire, I barely know how to express my appreciation. It is only with his formidable professional skills and brilliant sense of humor that I got this book to the finish line. He validated that I was a good enough writer to pursue publishing in the first place, and then gave me the guidance and confidence to get it done.

My deepest appreciation to Trish and Chris Meyer, whose wisdom, insight and highly trained eyes insured that this book had the proper look and feel. Thank you so much for lending your collective genius to this creation.

Thanks to Jody Andino, Adelle Abrahams, my dear friend Frances, Tana Sackett, Mark Combes, Mary Nokes, John Van Alstine, Sean & Bernadette Scanlan, Annie Bellman, Michael Wood, Nancy Downey, Rod Drought, and

Rebecca Thompson who all made me feel like my stories brought them joy.

There are many other dear friends to thank who have given me psychic support in my quest to pursue a new creative avenue, especially Phyllis Kaye, Natalie Davis, Danny Hampson and the very visionary Marcia McCoy who told me "Taba, you are on your path and deep in the forest."

Finally the most special thanks go to my soulmate and life partner, Kevin McGrath, whose love, kindness, patience and passion for life and golf provided me the opportunity to live my dream. It is only because of his affection and generous spirit that I could have the time to write and be given the most enjoyable topic to write about—that being the whole country of Ireland full of beauty and engaging people—and some of the best golf on the planet.

CONTENTS

PREFACE

My mother used to say you make your own luck. Is that so? I had to find out. That made me a truth seeker at a very young age. My curiosity led me to discover Edgar Cayce, The Bhagavad Gita, Dostoyevsky, Samuel Beckett, and other obscure authors like Napoleon Hill. Is that a made up name or was that a real person? I wasn't sure back then, but the story was so powerful that it didn't really matter.

One thing I did know—books held great knowledge—and they took me to worlds beyond what I could see, hear and touch. I couldn't articulate it then, but I knew there was an interior and exterior world and they did not always square with one another. Why not? How to do this?

Early in this journey, I realized that I was in love with the idea of writing a book, but when the thought struck me, I didn't really have anything to write about. Life had to unfold.

I continued to believe in finding my bliss, which evolved into following my passion, which now makes me quite lucky. It took five decades to do it, but I finally met my true life partner, Kevin McGrath. Back in October of 2004,

I was running a charity golf event at The European Club in Ireland, and Kevin came to play in place of another generous golfer who paid the entry fee but couldn't fly over from the U.S. I learned a few key things—Kevin was born in Dublin, played off a 5 handicap, and his business card said he was a Golf Travel Consultant. File that card someplace important!

By spring of 2005 I decided to launch my own golf travel venture so I would have plenty of reasons to get back to Scotland and Ireland to play golf myself. My entire business plan consisted of using only 5-star hotels and getting a partner who knew the lay of the land and who would make sure I didn't screw up when it comes to tee times. There was just no margin for error.

I found the card and called Kevin. I was delighted when he said he would be all too happy to work with me. Through our arrangement, I learned that not only is Kevin a fine golfer, he is a fine person, with exceptional business acumen and a delightful personality. Fast forward to 2008, when the stars aligned for us to connect on a deeper level. That's when it hit me. This guy is truly magnificent. And with those long, gorgeous legs (which he flaunts), he is an absolute Stallion! Not only that, he treated me so well, I felt like a Princess. So there you have it—the Stallion and the Princess!

We have now traveled all over Ireland together (sometimes with our clients) and I have become quite familiar with many of Ireland's magical golf landscapes, from the trophy courses to the hidden gems. The Scots may have invented the game that we all play today, but since the Irish embraced the sport in the mid-1800s, they have created over 400 courses, including one third of the world's links courses; seven of them in the World's Top 100 Courses ranked by *Golf* magazine.

There is no doubt that every golf enthusiast must experience Ireland at least once in their lifetime, or else their CV is not complete! Especially the rare and precious links, which are by the sea, and often carved out of spectacular, rugged dunes. Here the soil is sandy and the turf is springy. You'll walk with your caddie instead of ride in a buggie. You'll breathe the fresh air and feel the sheer exhilaration of being on this ancient and verdant island nation. You'll be far from home, but you'll feel right at home.

For golfer and non-golfer alike, Ireland delivers so much beauty and such rich history, all in a land mass about the size of Maine, that you can barely scratch the surface of in a week or two. From the stunning Cliffs of Moher on the west coast of County Clare to Newgrange, the 5,000-year-old passage tombs and burial mounds just north of Dublin, and six million friendly Irish people to welcome you everywhere you go, you just have to see it for yourself.

I hope you will.
Soon.

In the meantime, please enjoy a preview of this magnificent land through my stories and photography.

HOLD MY HAND

June 5, 2010

The Cliffs of Moher (*Aillte an Mohthair*) are reported to be the most visited natural tourist attraction in Ireland with close to a million visitors annually.

They are magnificent. Staggeringly beautiful. Contrasted by green pastures, cows grazing, fields of buttercups, lichen covered stone walls; and then the sheer, abrupt heart-stopping drop—down down down to the Atlantic Ocean.

A car park full of busses, air full of languages, cameras full of snapshots—the wide assortment of faces forming a tapestry with flowing saris, teenage blubbery midriffs, and bikers in matching black leather with the bottle-orange-haired-pony-tailed guy also sprouting what looks like dreadlocks dangling from his pierced chin.

Formed 320 million years ago, during the age known as the Upper Carboniferous period when it was much warmer, what became the cliffs evolved when this area sat at the mouth of a wide river, where it was saturated by mud and silt, which eventually settled into the rock layers.

This powerful convergence of land and sea has also inspired stories like the "Leap of the Foals." Illuminated in the visitor centre—the story goes… When St. Patrick introduced Christianity to Ireland, some of the old magical rituals of the past were abandoned. This angered the Tuatha Dé Danann, who were the masters of magic. In protest, they used their magic powers to turn themselves into horses and they galloped to Kilcornan where they hid for centuries in the caves. Time passed and one day seven foals emerged from the caves. Legend has it that they were frightened by the bright daylight. They bolted and, while galloping along the edge of the cliff, met an awful fate. The spot is now known as Aillenasharragh, or "Leap of the Foals."

And so the Stallion and the Princess drifted up the hill to the right where a not-so-ancient tower stands, built in 1835 with the intent to develop the site for tourism…and then reversed to the left up the dirt path to the Nag's Head, where one can't help but notice the signs asking "Do you need to talk?" and offering a 24/7 phone number.

I asked him what this meant and the Stallion informed me that, "Unfortunately there are about 15 suicides a year at the Cliffs of Moher." The mere thought took my breath away.

And then, while walking along the treacherous path just inches from the cliff edge, my Stallion said: "Take my hand—I don't want to lose my Princess," as he told me that yet another 15 or so people accidentally lose their lives each year—taken by surprise with a strong gust of wind.

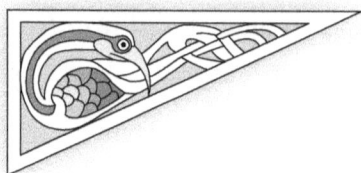

MOISTURISH

June 6, 2010

You all know why Ireland is called the Emerald Isle, right? Yes, of course you do—as the frequent rain produces a million shades of green as far as the eye can see in every direction. That said, I have just experienced the most delightful week-long stretch of sunshine and pleasant temperatures made even more perfect by a gentle breeze.

In general, the climate here is considerably milder than most countries at this latitude. In fact, the land mass that is Ireland sits at the confluence of four different air currents including the Gulf Stream and is further influenced by the ocean currents. When the warm air rises above the colder air of other currents, the convection produces condensation, which form the clouds and down pours the rain.

Today a gentle "intermittent-wiper-speed" rain returned and although some locals cancelled their golf, when Kevin and I arrived in the car park of Lahinch Golf Club for a bowl of soup in the clubhouse, three ladies were maneuvering their 'Powakaddy' trollies and sorting out their hats and brollies (umbrellas). I caught the eye of the Lady Captain, and I asked her, "Are you coming in or just going out?"

She replied, "We're off now…it's better than before," and therefore good enough weather to play golf—so onward the threesome went, rather cheerily.

What I find so amusing is how the Irish have an endless way of describing the wet conditions: "it's closing in," or "it's breaking up," or "it's going around us," or "it's a soft rain," or "it's a lashing rain," or "it's bucketing down," or "the worst is over—*overhead!*" Or—as reported in today's *Irish Independent:*

> **Ulster:** A cloudy and increasingly dull day.
>
> **Connacht:** The rain will persist on and off throughout the day.
>
> **Munster:** Cloudy with outbreaks of rain, very heavy and thundery in places.
>
> **Leinster:** A dull day with outbreaks of increasingly heavy rain after a dry start.
>
> **Dublin:** The rain will become persistent and heavy in the afternoon.
>
> **Outlook:** Tuesday cloudy with showers or longer periods of rain. The rain will become locally torrential in the afternoon with a risk of thunderstorms. Wednesday will be mainly dull and breezy with outbreaks of rain, heaviest in western counties. It will become drier and perhaps a touch brighter over Northern Ireland.

And then, ta da! **Thursday** will be a fine day just about everywhere with **sunny spells**.

ONE SHEET AT A TIME

June 7, 2010

Thank goodness it is a rare thing to have to put your glasses on to flush a toilet in the States, but it is sometimes necessary in Ireland. This situation arises due to the European oh-so-modern flushing mechanism whereby a quarter-size metal circle split in two—one wee button for "number 1" and a slightly larger button for "number 2"—is what you must depress to flush it all away.

And this action must be taken with sincere authority, not hesitatingly, or you will have to wait for the mechanism to recycle and do it all over again with utmost conviction!

On some fixtures there is even a classier version of the mechanism—two separate buttons! One obviously larger... clearly designating a more serious amount of water and sucking action. You are thankfully spared the danger of breaking a fingernail—you could even indulge in the luxury of pressing with two fingers if you were so inclined.

Then there is the matter of the toilet paper—which is sometimes dispensed one thin sheet at a time. Forget about a 2-ply or 4-ply roll with tiny perforations separating the squares, and perhaps a spare roll that drops down automatically when the first one is used up.

The one-sheet-at-a-time dispenser is clearly designed to teach you frugality, in case you are disposed to being extravagant and pull down an extra sheet or two, you might feel a severe wave of guilt—but there is no stuffing them back up into that box.

I suppose that someday somebody will write a treatise on the evolution of the toilet right up to our most modern era, where in fact we have "smart" toilets that sense we have moved our behind (or they are pre-programmed to flush in a you-should-be-done-by-now amount of time) and they just flush away—sometimes rather violently, so you better hold on to your panties!

And then there are the over-the-top variety of toilets, that I have heard are common in Japan. Apparently known as "washlets," they come with a dazzling array of features arranged on a control panel. Available options are: automatic lid opening, seat warming, massage elements, deodorization, and a blow dryer. Advanced features on the most high-end toilets offer vibrating and pulsating jets of water, and even play music to relax the user's sphincter!

At the end of the day, aren't we just grateful to have indoor plumbing?

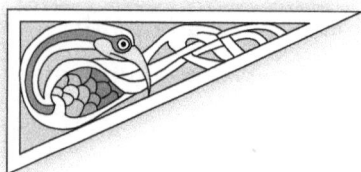

SURGERY IN THE SURGERY

June 14, 2010

Being a big fan of Sherlock Holmes stories, I am acquainted with the fact that in the 19th century, where doctors conducted their private practice was called The Surgery. Well, it is still called that here in Lahinch. There is a smallish sign on the outside of the converted house declaring: Medical Centre. But the more assuring, also smallish, bronze sign informs: Dr. Michael Kelleher and below his name, the following:

M.B.D.C.H.D.Obs,C.F.P.M.I.C.G.P.M.R.C.G.D.

No kidding. And then, the comforting: Diploma in Practical Dermatology, as I am about to have a little growth on my chest removed, that during my exam last week, was declared "not suspicious." I had noticed it changed texture in the last week or so and needed to be looked at. So today is the removal of the thing to be sent away for biopsy. Seaside village doctor or not, he was not taking any chances!

When I came for my consult a week ago, with just one day's notice, there was no requirement to download and fill out my forms in advance, or show up a half hour before my appointment to get all this paperwork done. My name, address, and birth date were simply handwritten on a note-pad and that was it. I was checked in.

After 45 minutes in the Waiting Room, I was shown in to the spartan doctor's office. It had a computer, but that was the only modern piece of equipment to be seen, until the very genial doctor arrived and used his sophisticated digital camera to take a photo of the bothersome growth, so he could show it to me in magnified detail.

It was determined to remove it the following week—the procedure including "a stitch or two." This time I had a full hour to wait before being shown into The Treatment Room, affording me ample opportunity to observe the homey environment.

The flying pig, fish and butterflies, suspended from the ceiling were kept company by the three giant ladybugs attached to the bright green doorframe. A rustic hobbyhorse with red eyes and hoofs, and a basket of plastic toys and stuffed animals dominated a corner of the room. A hodge-podge of photographs and original paintings decorated the pale yellow walls—with charming subjects like a horse being shod, another plowing a field, and a delightful scene of three blue-jean-clad lads riding bareback. One small photo of a frecklefaced girl in affectionate embrace with her stately horse revealed an equestrian passion, perhaps that of the doctor's daughter?

With a diagnosis of Actinic Keratosis, I left stitched up and told I'm in no danger—grateful that it was nothing more serious. We'll have results back in perhaps 21 days, but I'll have no anxiety about it. Elementary my dear Watson!

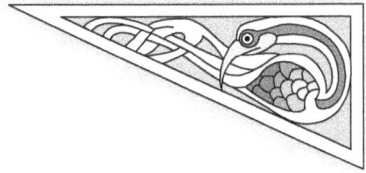

WAKING TO THE WHINNY

Morning, June 16, 2010

This morning I awoke to the sound of nearby horses whinnying. What a magical way to greet the new day. The curtains were drawn but I could picture them romping around in the field across from our front door; and the vision drew me into a conscious state of happiness.

They say every day is a brand new day—nowhere is it more true than here in Liscannor. Today, a thick mist is making the shoreline across the bay completely indistinguishable. The grey water looks endless.

And now, just a couple of hours later, the sun is bright; puffy white clouds give character to the sky, and the sea is sparkling with dazzling diamonds riding on the strong tidal current.

With the brightness, comes a bit of wind—as if moving in step with the flow of the water. Little fishing boats are heading out to sea, from the equally little Liscannor harbour.

To the east are the dunes of Lahinch Golf Club with the rooftops of the village shimmering as they rise up beyond the shore of the links.

Lazy gulls drift by, over the water, while smaller dark birds swoop and dart hither and to, over the grassy fields—all searching for their morning meals.

The reddish brown cows, generally chomping away every evening in the field to the west, are nowhere to be seen this morning.

Over the years people have asked me: "Do you have any animals?"

"No, I travel too much," is my stock answer.

Truth be told, I don't want the responsibility of looking after a house-bound pet. But I always thoroughly enjoy the rhythm of the animals around me whenever I am in the countryside.

Soon the sun will be high overhead and the bay will take on several luminous shades of azure blue…the diamonds now dancing in the waters to the west as they float out to the Atlantic Ocean.

The idyllic and ever-changing view calls to mind the famous P.G. Wodehouse quote:

"It was a morning when all nature shouted 'Fore!'"

LOVE IN LISCANNOR

Evening, June 16, 2010

L ove—as in the four-legged variety—is on display here in Liscannor in a most dramatic way! In fact, while driving up the road to our house, we were stunned when we saw a gorgeous pinto on a high mound—towering over the stone wall.

Whoa! Hold your horses! Stop! Back up! Luckily I had my camera with me, but did not dare to get out of the car, in case the horse might gallop away. He stood majestically as if a monument. Mane blowing in the sea breeze.

Performing in the lead role of his own movie, he posed—so statuesque. I was mesmerized by his beautiful coat of chestnut and white—and then he turned just so and I could see his, er, gigantic reproductive member dangling—majestically too!

Like of bolt of lightening—he was off into the field to find the brown mare.

There are two fields side-by-side, separated by an old stone wall—a piece of it missing now, as one brown horse knocked off a few stones when jumping over it…leaving his companion alone in the field directly across from our front door.

Now there were three horses romping around in the adjacent field—with quite a dance going on while the jumper contested for the small mare (is she in season?), who was already being pursued by the pinto. The lone horse on our side stood steadfastedly by the stone wall—in horsey dejection?

Although I tried to approach slowly and quietly with my camera, they all stopped to watch me! After a long pause, they went back to nuzzling and romping around, as I crept closer hoping they would continue to ignore me.

And then *pow*! The jumper kicked the pinto to improve his position and dominate the mare. I have never seen this kind of violent, but obviously natural behavior firsthand. Now I am wishing I had a video!

The three go romping to a faraway corner of that field, abandoning the lone horse who whinnies and snorts and trots in circles—seemingly frustrated at being left behind.

It is one thing to observe horses in their barns and quite another thing to see them on the loose—well, sort of on the loose. In any case, they are romping, cavorting, performing some mating rituals, being aggressive, acting curious, looking forlorn, and displaying a whole range of horsiness. And I have found no less than four new reasons to love Liscannor.

HAIRY ROCKS

June 17, 2010

Like my love affair with the giant granite boulders surrounding me in Scottsdale, Arizona, I have a fascination with the stones—especially the stone walls that define the landscape of County Clare.

What is this soft green hairy-looking growth all over the rough-hewn rocks that form our western wall? The one separating us from the field of grazing cows with the castle ruin rising in the distance.

It appears to be some kind of moss that must thrive on rocks—rocks that have endured years of Atlantic storms. Along with their irregular shapes and glowing lichen, the rocks form a crazy quilt of grey, green and white. They are visible from every window on that side of our house; but they create a whole new world when viewed from just inches away.

According to the book *Irish Stone Walls* by Patrick McAfee, the walls *live* and change with the season, and in summer come alive—some sprouting wild flowers. Now I am even more curious to see what happens as the days roll on. McAfee also says, "Some dry stone walls deserve to be listed as national treasures." I am instantly aware that I do treasure these walls.

Fronting our view to the bay and wrapping around the eastern side of our lawn, which is now mowed but dotted with buttercups and daisies, is a lower wall that looks to be built of Liscannor slate. Some of the slabs are nearly three inches thick by as much as two feet wide. The wall stands almost three feet high, with the lower slabs laid horizontally and the top foot or so with standing slabs at a jaunty angle—creating a very jagged top edge.

I first became aware of how famous the Liscannor stone is while stopping in at the Visitor Center at the Cliffs of Moher. This flagstone is particularly dark—myriad shades of grey to black. Apparently, before World War I, quarries thrived here and the thick slabs were used locally for floors, walls, paths; and even as roofing material. The stone kept the small Liscannor port very busy as shipments went regularly to London and Liverpool.

Up close, where I love to get my nose, I smell the sea. And I can see the fossil traces of marine animals or plants from millions of years ago. They speak to me, these rocks.

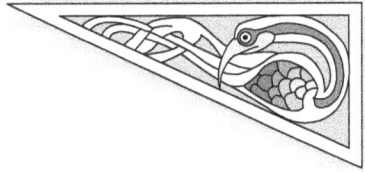

EEEK, A MOUSE!

June 18, 2010

Yep, this is truly country living. Last night after we ate a chicken casserole in the dining room, I was clearing the table and bringing dishes into the kitchen.

Just a few steps from the sink—*EEEEK!*—I saw the creature scramble behind the terracotta bread canister nestled in the corner of the counter…well, let's say I mainly saw its tail. That was enough!

"Kevin!!! Come in here!! I saw an…an animal…it went behind the bread thingy."

Okay, says he, I'll get him.

Good says me—I'm outta here!

Luckily, there are French doors to the kitchen so we could lock the bugger in there. Kevin set some traps (I guess—I didn't stick around to watch). Funny, I had just noticed the tiny traps under the sink earlier in the morning while trying to clean out that cabinet.

I thought the rickety-looking traps could be thrown away with all the other used-up Brillo pads and jumble of junky kitchen items...but no, Kevin said, "We'll use them."

Little did I know we would use them that very night.

As it was going on 8 PM and still very light outside, we headed out to play nine holes of golf. Instead of just going for a walk, we throw our golf clubs over our shoulders and amble around the Castle course, which is great fun—not the "monster" the Old course is considered to be.

We carry our bags, laugh a lot, take extra shots if we feel like it—not Kevin so much, he had six 3s in seven holes—and just missed an eagle on a short, but tricky par 4.

We came home to empty traps—well, I did not go look for myself. I just shut the French doors to the dining/living room, the bathroom door, the bedroom door and managed to forget about the critter—hoping he found his way out. The traps are now waiting for him under the sink and I will not, repeat not, be peeking in there to see if he is caught.

MUCH ADO
ABOUT SHOPPING

Morning, June 20, 2010

In one regard, Ireland is ahead of the U.S. in that you must bring your own bag to the grocery store. Today is Father's Day and while Kevin has filled in for a friend in a fourball, I decided to walk up to the nearby petrol station/ general store of Liscannor.

I had only four items in mind to bring home, but as I forgot to bring a bag, I just bought some Yop—a drinkable yogurt that helps the calcium supplement pills go down, and another banana-flavored "milkshake" with 570 mg calcium per bottle—one item for each hand.

Since I also carried my wallet and camera, I decided not to juggle too much more, as every step I take and wherever I fix my gaze, there is something worthy of a picture. Today, in a grassy area by the Top gas station/store were two pitiful-looking ponies, and one little girl walking with her cane-wielding grandma, stopped to pet one. Charming scene that I don't see when shopping at AJ's, Fry's or Safeway!

Grocery stores range from the gas-station-convenience-store variety, to the medium size SuperValu, up to the larger Tesco. We have to drive to the quaint market town of Ennistymon (*Inis Diomáin*) for the medium-size store, which surprisingly has an underground car park and escalator to the shopping level.

Oddly though, it costs a euro to unlock a shopping cart—but you do get it back at check out.

Another surprise—when the sign says "5 apples for €3," you have to buy five or else you don't get the special price, whereas in the U.S. if a sign says "5 Lean Cuisine meals for $10" (I would know!)…you can buy any number and each will be $2.

Of course you know that everything is in grams—like Denny pre-packaged 5 Honey Roast Ham Slices are 103 g. They do have a use-by date and quite a bit of nutritional information—including something I am not used to seeing on my honey ham slice package: "Energy 490 kj / 116 cal"—that is per 100g, or per slice 30kcal. The label also provides a Guideline Daily Amount section that says: "Typical Adult: Calories 2000 kcal, Fat 70g, Salt 6g." And to be as specific as possible, the following is provided: "Per Serving Calories 1.51%, Fat 1.1%, Salt 9.8%." More information than I know what to do with!

The St. Bernard Mature Red Cheddar Slice package goes even further to instruct: "Keep Refrigerated 0° c to +5° c.

Consume within four days of opening." Well, I didn't bother to read that until now, and I can't say I think I'm in any danger, having opened it a week ago or more.

That said, I have wrapped it in two layers of Cling Film—also called *Film étirable*, *Vershoudfolie*, and *Pellicola trasparente per alimenti*, which is enough to make me forget my name, never mind my bag!

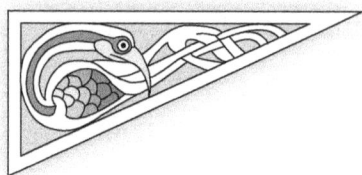

ULSTERMAN
TAKES THE TROPHY

Evening, June 20, 2010

What a superb Father's Day—especially for the man from Ulster, Graeme McDowell, winner of the U.S. Open—and for his father, Kenny, who was at Pebble Beach to witness the victory firsthand.

Kevin got an elaborate, sentimental card from me, and a nice phone call from his son in New York City. Kevin, Jr. is celebrating his first Father's Day with the birth of Alva, who is just six months old. Kevin's daughter, Nicola, celebrated with her husband and two young boys. A Sunday ritual while in Ireland, playing golf, was on the agenda for Kevin, who left rather early in the morning.

Much to my surprise and delight, we had enough time in the afternoon to drive up to The Burren Perfumery, advertised as the first perfumery in all of Ireland, and family-owned for 35 years. It was something I wanted to do since last September, when I learned about this special flower-filled,

mystical, rocky terrain simply known as The Burren
(*Boireann*).

I was keen to see if I could buy a bottle of a hand soap with
their famous Ilaun scent that I discovered while staying at
Doonbeg, where the room amenities include several of
Burren Perfumery products. We arrived at the perfect time
to have a scone and cup of tea, except the scones were all
gone. We settled for a divine piece of carrot cake instead.
Then we ambled through the enchanting herb garden, a
magical place with meandering pathways revealing a new
delight in every direction—like a bed of flowers planted
within the confines of an actual old wrought iron bed.

We timed our return to collect some wine from our fridge to
bring for lasagna dinner with Frances and her sister, Kalene,
who was down from Cork. The idea was, we would all watch
The U.S. Open final on TV together, but the leaders didn't
really get started until after 10 PM, which meant it would
be a very late night.

I'm sure I nodded off a few times before Kevin suggested
we go home to watch the end of the fourth round. After
having a bath around 11:30 PM, I revived enough to see
the Irishman hold on to his one-shot lead and win his first
major, becoming the next European to win The U.S. Open
since Tony Jacklin in 1970.

What a special treat to be here in Ireland, with my Irish
Stallion, who is both a father and passionate golfer. Of

course, in Stallionesque fashion, he had the stamina to stay up to 4:30 AM to watch the presentation ceremony and hear the acceptance speech live.

I imagine most of Ireland and all of the golf members of Portrush and Rathmore in Northern Ireland were wide-eyed and joyful while having a pint and watching their local Ulster hero on the telly. Soon G-Mac will bring home the hardware—which will certainly hold more than a few pints of Guinness!

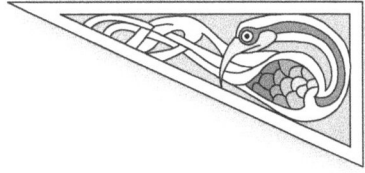

HOW'S THE CRAIC?

June 21, 2010

One of the most endearing components of Irish conversation is their charming colloquial expressions, such as, "How's the craic?" Pronounced crack, it simply means fun, goings on, or atmosphere. So if you hear, "The craic was great," it means they had a fun time. Or "She's great craic," it means she is a lot of fun to be with.

Roughly 100% of the Irish people I have met have a hilarious sense of humor and an infectious love of laughter.

Along with their often lilting voice, they continue to amuse me with the commonest of phrases like, "I'm just going to nip down to the bank (or a shop)…or "it's a doddle," meaning it's a cinch, it's easy.

Another common statement starts out, "Your man…" In fact, it's not really your man, it's *yer man*. It does not necessarily refer to someone you actually know—and it can even be someone despicable. This phrase can also apply to *yer woman* as well, which can be even worse, as *she* is certainly not mine!

Then yesterday Kevin asked me, "Not a dicky bird from David Brown?"

"A *what* darling?"

"Not a word?"

"Nope, not heard from him."

The golf match often has a "tenner" on it. Everything else is "no bother."

Here's a glossary of other common words and expressions:

Dosh—money.

Slagging me?—making fun of me?

Giving out—giving me a hard time.

Go way—no way, really? You can't mean that?

I'm not joking you!—I'm not making this up!

It's gas—it's wild, it's crazy, it's amazing, it's astonishing.

Absolutely brilliant—very cool, very clever.

Feck it—er, you can figure that one out on your own.

READY TO BE BOPPED

June 22, 2010

Eek A Mouse! turns out to be just the beginning! Eeek #1 didn't last very long, but we were smug too soon, as Eeek #2 and Eeek #3 appeared as a duo one morning, a day or so later. Oh cute. A matched pair.

"*Kevin...!!!* There's two of them! I see two of them!"

In to the kitchen runs Kevin, as I stay stuck in my high bar chair that I sit on while using my laptop, watching them scurry under the dishwasher.

"They're in there! *Get Them!!*"

Okay, now we mean business. Kevin put out three traps, close to the dishwasher, but in full view of me, who does not, repeat *does not,* want to see the bothersome critters in or out of a trap!

Now the day goes by with no more sightings but come the next morning—I can see through the French doors to the kitchen—there is a grey blob obscuring one of the traps.

Oh yuck. I don't want to even go in there with that dead thing (it is dead, isn't it?) lying there.

Don't ask me if our traps (small spring-loaded deals) are the ones called "Little Nipper." All I know is when Kevin tries to load a wee piece of cheese as bait, he curses a lot when the things keep snapping on him. Neither of the mice took the bait, but lo and behold, one of them appeared in the living room! "Eeek eeeek eeeeeck" I screamed when I saw him out of the corner of my eye just as I put a blanket down on the floor to do some stretches.

"Kevin!!!"

Okay, now it really is war on these troublemakers.

Kevin keeps saying, "I've only seen them in the winter when they come in from the cold."

"Well, sweetheart, they have moved into our nice cozy house—and it is, technically, summer."

I'm not sure who surprised who more—but one of the critters just ran out into the middle of the floor—as if to say, "I'm ready to be bopped."

Kevin dashed away to get something to bop him with, and bop he did. I didn't stick around to see him unceremoniously thrown into the trash can.

"Um, honey, could you please throw out the trash *now?*" That's Eeek #2 gone.

And then, nerve of all nerve, Eeek #3 pokes his head out in the living room while we were having dinner in the dining room, on a level two steps above.

Kevin lurches out of his chair to find his bopper, but Eeek #3 eludes him…for the time being anyhow. No way will I stick around to watch any golf tonight on the telly in the living room.

G'nite and good riddance to ya, you little menace. May tonight you dine on cheese!

And oh, by the way, it turns out there was an Eeek #4 (the blob in the trap who I promptly put out of my mind as soon as he went into the trash) *plus* an Eeek #5 that I did not even know about. Thankfully Kevin did not tell me until we were home in Scottsdale that he bopped another little sneaky mouse hiding in the fireplace!

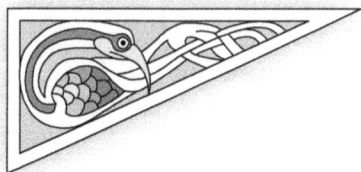

RHUBARB CRUMBLE

June 23, 2010

O ur very first dinner guests happen to be American! Steve and Beverly, who reside in Colorado, bought some land here in Lahinch high on the hill. They built a summer house a dozen years ago—made somewhat more modest than they might have wanted because of strict regulations by town overseers. Steve revealed, "They even gave us a hard time over the Wedgwood blue color we wanted to paint—probably because the English-sounding name didn't go down well."

It was a delight to have visitors to our house by the bay on such a perfect evening…especially now that we have gotten rid of the furry Eeek family. While having a glass of wine and taking in the view, Beverly pointed out the magpie—a gorgeous bird with distinctive black and white markings, apparently a member of the crow family, but much more beautiful, especially in flight.

Next we all marvelled at the castle ruin to the west, and I said to Beverly, "Oh I'd love to look through the telescope," (a fancy Bushnell on a tripod), "but so far the only image I can see is upside down!"

Kevin informed me earlier, "That is only to settle on the object and then you have to look through another lens to really *see* what you are looking at."

But I thought, *Oh, I'm just too short to see anything*, at which point Beverly removed the lens cover. Voila! No longer a black void.

Into the constantly changing panorama appeared a strange boat. The ever-observant Beverly pointed out, "That is a *currach*—they're very rare." My first sighting! These hand-made wooden boats are unique to the west coast of Ireland (and Scotland). This particular canoe-like boat was just big enough for two rowers. Apparently in olden days, they were covered in animal skins or hide, but newer ones most likely have a canvas covering. Hopefully by the time the next one floats by, I will know how to operate the goddamn telescope!

And now finally the main event...our chicken with mushroom and garlic sauce. It is no secret that I am not known for my cooking skills, but Kevin likes this dish so much, we have already made it five times in two weeks! The recipe is one I adapted from a little booklet I picked up somewhere for pork. How can you go wrong with olive oil, butter, garlic, shallots, sherry and *crème fraiche*? We like to think the extra calories are easy to justify with all the walking we are doing—mainly while trying to get a little white ball into a 4¼″ hole.

We finished off with Beverly's Rhubarb Crumble made with rhubarb grown in her own garden. What a coincidence that it is Kevin's favourite Irish desert. Not! The cheeky host asked her to make it.

But best of all is the slice we had left over for the next day. There was even just enough vanilla ice cream to help stretch the treat a bit more. Thanks Steve and Beverly. What day did you say you are returning in August?

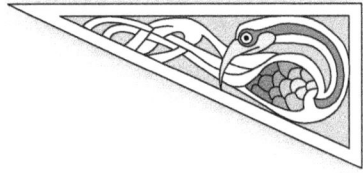

A TIME OF THE SIGNS

June 24, 2010

At last we had a reason to go up that windy back road to Ennistymon. This was to be the day we bought some welcoming flowers for the empty pots by our front door from a local farmer's nursery.

We headed out toward Lahinch (*An Leacht*)—although some newer signs have the spelling Lehinch, the Wikipedia site says: Lahinch is the anglicised form of *Leath Inse* and not related to *Leacht Uí Chonchubhair*. Recorded in *The Annals of the Four Masters* (or *The Annals of the Kingdom of Ireland*) as *Leith Innse*, which is a variant of the Irish word for a peninsula *leithinis* (half island), the name describes the village's location between the Inagh river and the sea. The ancient name for Lahinch, *Leacht Uí Chonchubhair*, which is still commonly used in Irish instead of the short-ened official name *An Leacht*, refers to the memorial cairn (*Leacht*) marking the burial place of one of the O'Connor chieftains, who were the ruling clan of the district of *Corco Modhruadh Iartharach*. Nowadays, the town name is gener-ally spelled "Lahinch," but a selection of road signs in the area use the spelling "Lehinch." Pronunciation of the placename is somewhat between the two spellings.

At the fork in the road, we came upon the rustic "Pony Trekking" sign, which cannot help but catch your eye. Bright red lettering with a primitive blue horse, hand-painted on a small piece of whitewashed wood, must call to the holidaymakers that come to visit the idyllic west coast in County Clare. No need for the Irish spelling!

In Ireland, cities, towns and villages are all signposted in both English and Gaelic language. It is another fascination for me—how the archaic looking and sounding words are translated into the modern spelling. Coupled with driving on the left side of the road, the signs are a constant reminder that I am in an ancient and foreign country.

We ambled up the single track road, passing through a tunnel of trees—aware that somewhere along this stretch was the "pony farm," but we were not to be distracted from our mission to buy flowers. Kevin thought he remembered a sign being on the left around a bend, but alas, there was no sign of a sign, which is not a good sign.

The nursery must be no more, another casualty of the economic meltdown that has devastated this proud little country. With a dip in our mood, we circled into Ennistymon to a place where we bought a cheery mixture of red, pink, white and purple flowers.

Once home, I hastily filled the empty pots, eager to send the world the signal: "We're home! And you are welcome!" Always a good sign.

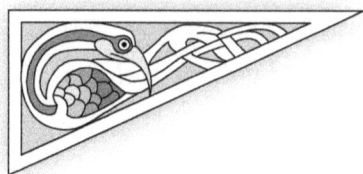

LIFE IN A VACUUM

June 25, 2010

Reading the newspaper in Ireland is not only informative, but sometimes highly amusing. In a story about BP, the writer reports that due to the big oil spill disaster in the Gulf, the share price has dropped so significantly that it may be a good time for investors to "hoover them up!"

Now it so happens that my first and only vacuum cleaner for about thirty years was a Hoover, so I found it quite comical to learn "to hoover" is a common verb in the UK and Ireland. It is rather like calling all tissue Kleenex, but that is what we do in the States.

My trusty Hoover was a heavy metal government-green sort of affair and came along with me everywhere I lived from Capitol Hill to Dupont Circle to Georgetown and points beyond D.C. I don't remember at what stage it went to Hoover heaven, but I think it died when the cord was frayed beyond repair or replacement.

Hoover was apparently such a dominant brand over here that it became synonymous with the act of vacuuming.

In Kevin's case, he is particularly proficient at hoovering up his food. In fact, his food disappears so fast, that I am often giving him what I can't eat. And I don't even bother to put it somewhere on his plate, I load directly onto his fork for maximum hoovering suction action.

My powerful, bagless, upright Irish model has lots of other on-board tools and is especially expert at hoovering up chocolates, cookies, and rhubarb crumble…in case you are in need of having anything sweet hoovered up!

DISCOVERY
AT DOOLIN

June 26, 2010

The most blustery wind we have had to date has churned up white caps in the bay. What must be a 4-club wind will give Kevin all the challenge that he relishes in his match later today.

Me, I'm happy to be warm and cozy, write a story, go for a walk, check on my horsey neighbors, and maybe try planting what we bought on Saturday at "the nursery."

Some friends who love to garden said, "Oh you must go up to our favorite nursery—it's on the road to Ballinalacken Castle." So yesterday we drove up to the small fishing village of Doolin (*Dúlainn*) by the Cliffs of Moher road along the coast. When we passed by it on our way back from The Burren recently, Kevin mentioned that this is the absolute epicenter of Traditional Irish music. People flock from all over the world to hear and play the drinking songs and ballads that Ireland is famous for. I even snapped a picture of three harpists playing last Sunday as we wended our way through the crowded village of Kilfenora (*Cill Fhionnúrach*) during the little town music festival.

Doolin Cave is another great attraction—saved for a future day. For surfers, Doolin is a major destination due to a reef break which creates the biggest waves in Ireland. "Aill Na Searrach" was even featured in the movie *Waveriders*!

Without any directions or even a name or phone number, we set out on our mission to find the nursery, which turned out to be a truly magical garden. Up a windy road, we passed a cemetary full of ancient celtic crosses, several quaint cottages and finally came upon a subtle sign indicating we had arrived at our destination. After carefully negotiating a slippery cattle guard, we spotted a slightly built man painting a wooden flower box.

Not wanting to disturb his meditative mood, I ventured, "What a gorgeous shade of purple," being an absolute lover of all things purple. With a twinkle in his eye, he explained, "Purple is such a beautiful color in one's garden, especially in winter time."

I told this gentle soul, "I'm looking for some plants for our tiny rock garden at our house in Liscannor. I have no clue what I'm doing, I'm just trying to get started somehow."

"I'll be happy to help you," he said with a smile. "My name is Matt. Follow me."

He escorted us around the corner of his understated contemporary house to what revealed a magnificent formal garden of enormous proportion. This was no ordinary nursery, but a living work of art.

Both humble and proud, Matt told us, "I planted everything you see."

He seemed genuinely delighted to stroll around and point out things common and exotic. Just about the only thing I recognized was hosta, which I love, but didn't think could survive in our excessively windy corner.

"Okay, let's go over to where I keep the growing containers," Matt said, steering us to the other side of the house. We wound up choosing six small pots—all perennial—some for ground cover and a few other more colorful things.

Although I wanted more plants and larger ones to make our little plot of land by the front door look lush and "done," Kevin, who has never had a passion for any kind of plants, said, "We can watch the small ones grow and that will be part of the fun!"

I'm hoping the wind calms down enough for me to plant our velvety soft little Lamb's Ear, the Yellow Sedum, the 'Mavis Simpson,' which Matt says is in the geranium family (hallelujah!—a plant I am familiar with) and a few other things "that are good by the sea."

When we heard Matt say we'd chosen something called "Mavis" Kevin and I broke into giggles. "Mavis!" we echoed, both of us laughing because that is what we call our GPS system for travelling around in America.

But I reminded Kevin, "Mavis needs to take a geography class! She doesn't know where she's going half the time!"

You see, Mavis has not been programmed with the new roads (she's a year 2000 model) and frequently tells us we are "Off Route…Recalculating."

In Ireland, off route is where we generally want to be!

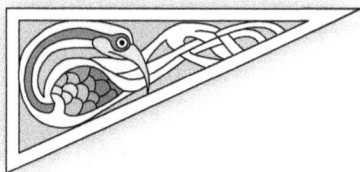

IRISH-Y IRISH

June 27, 2010

There is a pier-side restaurant in the charming, picturesque town of Kinsale (*Cionn tSáile*), promoted as the "gourmet capital of Ireland," called Fishy Fishy. There can be no doubt that they specialize in seafood—and everything they serve is caught locally. They pride themselves in being "committed to prioritising the core indigenous ingredients of Irish Cuisine."

Another indigenous ingredient of Ireland that enchants me is their names—that is, people *and* places.

As my own name always stirs up curiosity, I thought I would sort of blend in here after encountering so many women (in person or in print) with names like: Grainne, Moira, Moya, Oonagh, and Orla. I fit right in, don't I? *Taba.*

Nope, not a chance. It is always the same questions like: What kind of name is that? Where does it come from? How do you spell it? Then the usual mispronunciation, even when I spell it Tay-ba "like the River Tay in Scotland," they struggle. Eventually, after we go through the embarrassment of the gentle correcting phase, finally they get it and I am just Taba. Whew, but it takes some effort.

It also takes effort to learn the more exotic names here too—like Aoife, Eithne, Fionnuala, Maeve, Niamh, or Sinead or Siobhan; and for the men, Cian, Daithi, Diarmuid, Donogh, Enda, Finbarr, Niall, or Ruari. Thank goodness there are the more common aboriginal names like Aidan, Ailbe, Kieran, Liam, and Sean for the men; and Claire, Deirdre, Fiona, Frances, Mary, and Shannon for the women.

But take an easy sounding name like Kevin and put it in the Gaelic spelling—*Caoimhín*—and I am floundering.

Which brings me back to Fishy Fishy, where you can taste some gorgeous Irishy fish like Hake, Plaice and Skate. Or the eternally popular bass, cod and salmon. No Gaelic dictionary required!

A DRIVING HABIT

July 1, 2010

When Kevin and I got home to Liscannor from our three-and-a-half-hour drive back from Dublin, we had our dinner around 8 PM. As nightfall was still a long time away, we went for a walk up toward the castle ruin.

First we turned left and passed by Holland House, which Kevin believes is where John P. Holland (1840–1914) was born—famous for having invented the submarine. It is an unassuming whitewashed cottage with several original window panes of thick, antique glass. Two black, massively heavy and equally antique looking anchors are leaning up against the wall on either side of the front door.

Kevin revealed, "The street used to be called Castle Street, but has been renamed Holland Street."

Oh, that made sense, the twentieth-century town fathers wanting to honor their famous son.

A little farther up the hill is the imposing castle ruin. Nearby is a school for young children—it is a modest, low-slung single story building. The castle ruin towers over everything, rising five stories, and due to its position on the cliff, is visible for miles in every direction. It is described in *County Clare: A History and Topography*, 1837, by Samuel Lewis as: "formerly of great strength and the residence of the O'Conors."

Beyond that is a cluster of "Holiday Homes" that people rent on a weekly basis.

When we reached that point, Kevin said, "I think this is a holiday home for nuns…" And this part really cracked me up when he added, "because those are nuns' cars parked in front." In actual fact, they were very small Ford hatchbacks, one of many models not sold in America.

They are larger than "Smart Cars" but not by much. Probably perfect for negotiating the narrow country roads of Co. Clare, and probably perfect for nuns.

All of these houses are on the bluff with magnificent panoramic views of Liscannor Bay. Although little more than a quarter of a mile from our house, as the crow flies, the bluff is actually the start of what becomes the Cliffs of Moher, which are dramatic beyond belief.

Anyway, when we came back down the hill, one of the cars was gone—so away they sped—to do whatever nuns do on holiday.

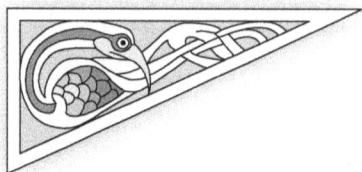

KNOCKING AROUND
THE ISLAND

July 2, 2010

We were leaving Dublin yesterday and I got out the map to see our route. It started on the M4 after we grabbed a bowl of potato and leek soup and toasted sandwich at The Deadman's Inn. Our three-and-a-half-hour journey would take us west through Leixlip and Maynooth, onto the M6, passing Fardrum on the way to Athlone. After crossing both the River Shannon (the longest river in Ireland) and the River Suck (no kidding), we would then find ourselves on the N6, where we would pass Cappataggle on the way to Loughrea. We would not travel on to the famous Athenry, but go south on the N66 to Gort.

Now Gort is nowhere near Gorteeny or Gornahoo. But Gornahoo is near Twomileborris, which reminds me of passing Sixmilebridge on the way to another famous town of Limerick. Not-so-famous is the village of Ninemilehouse.

What tickles me even more is New Twopothouse Village, which prompts a search of more funny names like: Spiddle,

Coolboy, Cloonfad, Sneem, Bweeng, Inch, Gneevgullia, Deelish and Dripsey—and Horse & Jockey. Yep. That's a village on the map. Then there is The Hand Cross Roads, which is a town, like Irishtown. Not nearly as exotic sounding as Emlaghnamuck.

You might also be surprised to know that in Ireland there are some very familiar sounding names such as: Hollywood, Baltimore, Westport and Newport; and there is even a Coney Island. But one wonders, what country are we in when we see places like: Labasheeda, Thurles, Glinsk or Carrick-On-Suir. I don't think you'd guess Ireland, if I queried you.

Those of us who love links golf are very keen to play at Ballybunion, and we have heard of Bally-this and Bally-that (the common prefix being derived from the Gaelic phrase *Baile Na* meaning "the place of"), but some have a comical ring like Ballyragget, Ballynacally, or Ballylooby.

Ireland being an island, there are lots of *heads* ringing the jagged coast—a sampling being: Old Head, Cod's Head, Crow Head, Hog's Head, Lamb's Head, Loop Head, Streek Head, Toe Head, Ram Head, Mine Head, and Hag's Head—not far from us at the Cliffs of Moher.

Some of the most Irish-y of all are: Knockaderry, Knocknagree, Knockagashel, Knocklong, Knocklomena, Knocknahilan and Knockanarrigan. But somebody must have gotten knocked upside the head and gotten things

completely backwards—naming their town Carrowmoreknock!
Actually there are oodles of towns called something-knock.
And then there is just plain Knock.

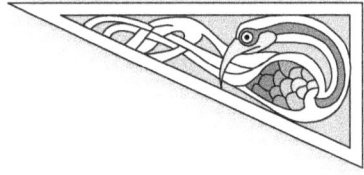

TIKI BAR

July 3, 2010

Yesterday was so cold, windy and rainy that I didn't stand a chance to get our potted plants into the ground. The lichen-covered rocks in the garden still await the interplay of color and texture huddled in the corner, sheltered from the Atlantic gusts. Maybe I should plant a turbine instead?

Although we had signed up to play in the newly organized Friday evening "Social, Mixed" golf at Lahinch, I wondered aloud to Kevin, "Will we have to play in this weather?"

He said, "It will not be up to just us—if the other two people signed up to play at 5:30 PM want to play, then we have to play."

And play we did. I had on five layers and looked like I was bound for the North Pole. The other three golfers had on shirts and shorts and looked like they were headed to a tiki bar in the South Pacific. I kid you not. And it's not just because I live in Arizona, I think I was just born with thin blood.

We fortified ourselves with a bowl of soup and packed our waterproofs into our golf bags. Thankfully, the rain eased up and we went out to play with Margorie and Brendan. Although we played in a 3-club wind at Portmarnock on Wednesday, this wind felt more fierce. Especially on the first hole, which is all uphill to a small elevated green. And every hole after that, the wind was a constant.

On the par-3 eleventh hole, Brendan, playing off a 9 handicap, shaking his head and smiling, walked up on the tee box and simply said, "I don't know." His tee shot was in play, but none of our balls stayed on the green. The wind was a factor on every putt as well.

During my last round at Lahinch, I birdied this hole, so I had a bit more confidence. I think we escaped with a 5, but for the other team, it was a blank on the card, with Stapleford scoring.

With all the battling of the elements, one of the nicest things about playing with Irish golfers is that I never feel as though I am battling with them personally. There may be a fiver, a pint, or a social-mixed-winner title (and some euros!) on the line, but instead of tension, there are smiles, stories, and camaraderie as we walk to each tee and play each hole.

It is a pure links golf experience. There are no range finders, no GPS. The yardage is usually on a marker on each tee box, and there *may* be a 150-yard post on the edge of the fairway, or some embedded disks indicating 200, 150 and

100 yards to the green. You have to use your imagination and work it out for yourself what club to use. A white stone may be your aiming point on a blind hole. On the famous "Dell," the blind par-3 fifth at Lahinch, the stone is moved every day as the hole is cut in a different part of the green.

The more I play here, the more I marvel at the unique challenge that each hole presents. On a calm day, it is a magical stage of 18 dramas. Add the wind, and you feel more like a warrior—and a winner just for getting around the course.

Take me to Trader Vic's! Make mine a Mai Tai.

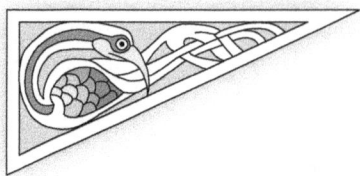

SUNDAY SHOCK

July 4, 2010

We got to the SuperValu a few minutes before 6 PM intending to buy some chicken breasts, garlic, a green vegetable, and a few other things. We took the back road just in case the throngs of surfers created a traffic jam leaving the beach at Lahinch.

Imagine my shock when we discovered that the shelves were empty. I mean completely bare!

"Sweetheart, where's all the food? This is the way it looks when a blizzard would hit D.C. and it's not even snowing!"

Kevin was a bit amazed too. "What's going on? It's not like you celebrate the Fourth of July here in Ireland," I said as we scurried through the produce section to get the chicken.

"Oh no! There's no chicken. How can there be *no* chicken," I wondered aloud in exasperation.

"Okay," Kevin said, "Let's get pork chops."

Nope. No pork chops. We wound up with a package of Angus Beef Pasta Medallions (there were only two left) and a container of Italian Style Bolognese Pasta Sauce.

"Sweetheart, let's get some Parmesan."

"They don't sell Parmesan at this store," Kevin stated matter-of-factly, "but we can try one other little shop on the way home." Luckily we found a wedge of Parmigiano-Reggiano. How fresh it was, I don't know.

After our little meal, we finally got around to me getting behind the wheel of Kevin's BMW with right-hand drive and left-hand shift. We moved the seat up as far as possible so I could get the clutch in. No problem, I learned on a stick, and slipped the car right in to first gear.

I steered the car through the iron gates and took the road up toward the castle ruin. Kevin got his own big shock when I tried to be oh-so-careful about staying on the left side of the road. "*Look out!* You nearly took the left side of the car off ," he screamed.

"I did *not!* Now you know how it feels when you are driving!"

When we came to a dead end and I needed to turn the car around, I put it in reverse and Kevin went crazy again. "You nearly hit the fire hydrant!"

"I wasn't going to hit it. Calm down!"

There was a car parked on the side of the road, and Kevin freaked out again. "*Stop!* You're going to hit that car!"

"I am *not*. Will you stop screaming at me?"

"You don't have to drive down the left side of the road. You just drive right down the middle, and you only move over if another car is coming."

"But there are all these blind hills. I don't want to be in the middle when some car comes flying over the crest!"

I drove back home, not wanting to continue this experiment. I didn't even feel confident about driving to Ennistymon to get groceries.

With Kevin leaving on Friday to join seven golfers missing their 8th (meaning Kevin could fill in to make up the two foursomes), the car may just sit there for the entire five days. The coach driver will pick up Kevin on the way to the airport to collect our clients when they arrive from Canada, and he will travel with them until the 8th guy arrives.

Who knows, maybe I'll shock us both and get my nerve up to try it again. Kevin's car is a gutsy eight-cylinder sedan (called a Grand saloon over here) and unless you understand how narrow and twisty the roads are, my apprehension may sound silly. This powerful car also sits very low to the ground, and it is hard to see around the stone walls and hedgerows when you come to a bend in the road.

Or perhaps I should just hire my own coach and driver for the week. After all, what's good for the Stallion is good for the Princess!

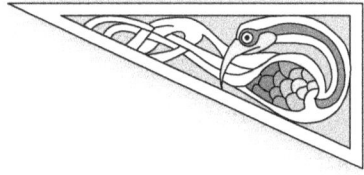

A DREAM FIELD

July 6, 2010

We spent the entire afternoon yesterday at the JP McManus Invitational Pro-Am; staged at the Robert Trent Jones Sr. (1906–2000) course at Adare Manor in County Limerick. It is the last major course he designed, and was opened in 1995. The two-day event, inaugurated in 1990, is played every five years—and has raised a staggering €55 million for dozens of charities in the midwest of Ireland.

Kevin, cleverly remembering a back road, skirted around the miles of cars in a massive 2+ hour back-up to get into the pretty little village of Adare (*Áth Dara*). We parked on a grassy lot and followed the stream of people through a field of waist-high barley, walking single file along the giant tractor tracks. It was an almost mystical scene, with the stately Adare Manor Hotel finally coming into view from behind a wall of trees, as we golf pilgrims emerged from a tan sea of wavy stalks of heady grain.

"I'm hungry, darling," I cried. "Can we find something to eat?"

"Me too," Kevin said. We threaded our way through the throngs of people, until we spotted The Dog House. After inching along in the lengthy queue, we grabbed our not-so-hot-hotdogs and hurried out on the course.

The record-breaking crowd of more than 40,000 came to watch defending champion Padraig Harrington, reigning U.S. Open champion, Graeme McDowell, and a dream field of 13 of the 16 top players in the world. Yes, including Tiger Woods. We were part of the enormous gallery on the 12th green, where we did glimpse him on his way to a painful 79. On this testy 7,453 yard layout, in windy conditions, Harrington finished with a 76, we later learned, taking a double bogey on the treacherous 18th.

Much to my surprise and delight, we got to see my D.C. hometown hero, Fred Funk, tee off on the 167-yard par-3 sixteenth. First shot in the water. Second shot just a few feet from the flag. In this festive atmosphere, Fred eagerly turned around and signed lots of hats for dozens of kids. This was when I realized, that oh, Tom Lehman was in the next group. Get ready!

The jolly crowd surrounding the tee box was full of cheeky amusement when Lehman consulted his caddie on what club to hit in the swirling wind, to carry the water to a narrow, heavily-bunkered green. They yelled in unison: "7-iron! 7-iron!"

When the 7-iron carried *over* the green, someone in the gallery yelled, " Fred Funk hit a 9-iron," to which Lehman quipped, "They better give him a drug test!"

With the page opened to Tom's photo, I got my outstretched program in his line of sight and said: "For a Scottsdale fan!"

My new "hometown" hero (who lives at DC Ranch, not far from me in Scottsdale, Arizona) took my program and while autographing his page, sweetened our little moment when he said, "The weather's much better here isn't it?"

"You bet it is," I agreed. We were both happy to be out of the broiling summer sun of the desert.

But perhaps the biggest hero of all for me was the one-legged amateur player, Manuel de los Santos, playing with Lucas Glover, who after knocking his bogey putt in with his rubber-footed crutch, was all smiles and bowed gracefully to the cheering crowd.

Last thrill of the day—walking down the 18th and seeing the crush of giggling girls trying to get their picture taken with Hugh Grant. And yeah—if you want to know, he really is kinda cute up close!

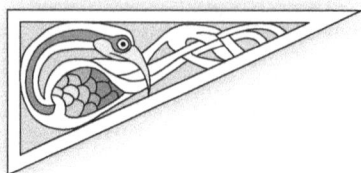

PANDEMONIUM
IN THE PASTURE

July 7, 2010

L ife here by the Liscannor Bay has a certain rhythm. The tide comes in. The tide goes out. The fishing boat motors to his lobster traps—the catch may be the key ingredient of "Liscannor lobster foie gras" at Vaughan's Anchor Inn?

Gulls glide and magpies swoop in search of food. The wind whips up. The wind calms down. A mist hangs. The mist rises. Clouds billow up. Clouds disappear. Tommy, a Clare native and our summer gardener, arrives with his ride-on mower and the lawn soon looks tidy.

The horses in the fields to the front of the house are convening at the stone wall. There are now three horses on the western side—a newcomer joins Chestnut and Pinto. And there's a different horse on the eastern side of the wall—a thoroughbred-looking bay with a white star. Pinto is especially curious about Star. They nuzzle each other across the wall—sometimes seemingly with mutual affection.

I can watch their empathic communication while I keep my distance, some 100 yards away from our bedroom window. There is an entire herd conversation going on out there that I don't understand, but am enraptured by.

When dinner time rolls around and Kevin and I share our meal, we have the magical and constantly moving panorama caressing us with candlelight and our favourite romantic music.

And then—OMIGOD—there is pandemonium in the pasture!! Five cows are charging toward our west window. The hairy rock wall separates that field from us, otherwise they could trample their way right into our living room! What caused this uproar?

"Quick Kevin, let's go watch them with the telescope!"

Which is silly, because they are romping around so fast, we can barely keep up with them.

"Look! They're over there!"

"Look! They're all the way over there now!"

"Look! He's humping her!"

We are falling over ourselves wondering what is going on with this wild confusion? Then they get into a cow huddle and sort things out. Throughout all this mayhem, the bigger cows are nonchalantly chomping away. We realize these are the baby cows, just having a game of cow rugby, or something like that.

Take it from me: When a bunch cows, even if just 300-lb. calves, start to stampede, it constitutes more than a modicum of curiosity. Thankfully, we can watch the Cow League penalty shootout from our private skybox suite!

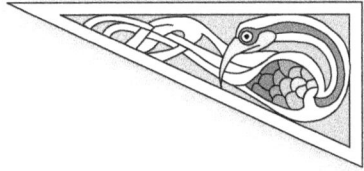

THE BUSTLE

July 8, 2010

The Bustle is not at all unique to Ireland, but this is where I first heard the word. In fact, it came up in the following story that Kevin told me, which took place when he was in his late teens:

Kevin and his young teammate, Pat Walshe, were playing in the quarterfinals of the Donabate Golf Club's Annual Fourball Matchplay Championship, against what could only be termed as "a pair of old codgers." They were at that time the current title holders of the event, but also former winners in several other years. The match was well poised with the young pretenders 2-up going to the 16th hole. Following two great shots to a difficult par-4 hole, Kevin's partner had two putts to win the match. As Pat was addressing his ball on the green, Codger No. 1 said very bluntly, "You aren't going to three putt, are you?"

And you guessed it. He did. Completely discombobulated, Kevin and his partner lost the final two holes to the defending champions, but fading light prevented them from going back to the first hole to start the "sudden death" playoff, and it was agreed to replay the full match the following day. Smarting from the very intentional "bustle" of the previous day, the young lads decided to be fully prepared for any such repeat "shenanigans" and beat the crafty competitors handily 6 and 5 (which means 6 up with 5 holes to play).

The next time the subject came up in conversation, it was the same night that we were having dinner with Frances and her sister while watching the U.S. Open final round on her big-screen TV. That's when Frances volunteered this cheeky example of a bustle when someone asked her, "Do you inhale or exhale on your backswing?" A question clearly designed to put you off your game.

A short time later, we drove up to Dublin and stayed over in John Flanagan's apartment near Portmarnock. John was a longtime friend, who used to stay with Kevin when he came down to Lahinch to play golf. I happened to pick up a book from John's living room shelf called, *Christy O'Connor – His Autobiography as told to John Redmond,* which provides examples of this kind of gamesmanship at the highest level in professional golf.

Now here is a world-class bustle involving none other than five-time Open Championship winner Peter Thomson as described by O'Connor while playing him in a tense quarter final of the PGA Match Play Championship at Turnberry in 1957. After the eighth hole when O'Connor went 1-up this is what happened:

"On we proceeded to the next tee. As I was about to make my swing, Thomson shuffled his feet. His white shoes stood out distinctively in an era when those of us less well-traveled or successful were wearing the staid but traditional black or brown shoes. I asked him to be still while I played. No further words were exchanged between us but on every green and on every tee I glanced disapprovingly at him. I wanted him to be in no doubt as to my feelings about his gamesmanship. But on the fifteenth tee he moved his white shoes once more, just when I was about to drive. I stepped away from my ball and walked towards him. I stared Thomson straight in the eye. 'Stand still while I'm addressing the ball.'"

This was just one of three incidents during that round that required the referee to be called to adjudicate. End result: O'Connor beat Thompson by two holes.

Moral of the story: Beware of the intentional bustle as it can often come back to bite you.

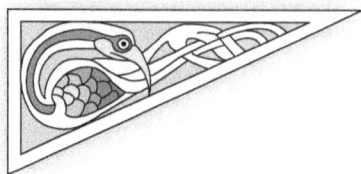

MYSTICAL MUSIC

Morning, July 9, 2010

The phone rings around 10 PM but I don't bother to even try to answer it—figured it is probably for Kevin. He had gone down to Egan's to meet Sean Scanlan for a pint. Nothing unusual about that.

What was unusual is, all of a sudden, I can hear Kevin's car pull up outside and I wonder why he's back so early. Turns out some musicians were getting ready to play traditional Irish music at Egan's and he's anxious for me to hear them— and yes, that was him calling on the phone to tell me about it and see if I was interested.

Kevin bursts in to the room and insists, "You really have to come down to Egans! This is a very unique thing—it might only happen once a year!" So yes, in fast-forward, I get myself dressed for going out, and get into the car—engine still running!

Was I ever in for a treat. There's nothing like live music, especially in such an intimate setting as a one-room pub. Tin whistle, banjo, accordion, guitar, a smallish drum called a *bodhrán* and violin were the instruments. The music is spontaneous and lively. The musicians ranged from a boy of about nine or ten up to young adults—that is, until the white-haired Master arrives. Kevin thinks it is the patriarch of the famous McPeake family of Belfast—a highly regarded teacher from a long line of traditional musicians—and apparently these are several of his students who have come to the summer music school in Miltown Malbay, just down the coast from us.

July is the time of the yearly Willie Clancy Music Festival—dedicated to the famous local piper, and includes lectures, classes and recitals in all the traditional Irish arts.

Without a word spoken, a chair materialises in the crowded pub. The older gentleman in the Donegal tweed waistcoat sits down with the circle of performers and a reverential hush falls over the room. He takes a whistle out of his pocket and begins to play. No one makes a move. We all just listen to the soulful sound of this airy instrument. This is it. Authentic stuff.

In perfect synchronicity, all the other musicians then come alive and the whole room is infused with exquisite energy. After another couple of songs, the maestro rises and leaves as ghost-like as he arrived.

Another well-known local musician, Mick Flynn, sits down and begins to sing and play his " knapsack guitar," a slender teardrop-shaped instrument with six strings like a more common guitar. We are all spellbound again. I am sure he continued on into the wee morning hours, as the pints continue to arrive.

And so I have witnessed "Our own Johnny Cash," as Sean called him. Magical. Heart-warming. Soul-touching. It warrants repeating: Authentic stuff.

POPULATION: 67

Evening, July 9, 2010

I heard Kevin say, "Liscannor (*Lios Ceannúir*) is a little fishing village of only 200 people." But I now know the population is only 67—not counting horses and cows!

When I stumbled into the treasure trove which is Egan's Books and Wine Too, little did I know that I would encounter the village historian. Patrick Egan is a third (or did he say fourth?) generation Liscannor resident. Believe he said his father came back from America to Ireland on a boat in 1904. With a hint of sadness, Patrick said he is the last of the Egan line.

The retired architect, who revealed he lived in London for twenty or so years, is now a combination book dealer and wine merchant. The hundreds of books lining the entire back wall pulled me in like a magnet. I had just walked down to the busy little harbour and then crossed the street to snap a photo of the whimsical bronze sculpture of John Philip Holland peering out of a submarine hatch—as if "emerging" near the entry of the Cliffs of Moher Hotel— thus my curiosity about Holland was in a high gear. Law of attraction at work here.

"Turns out," said Patrick, "Holland (1841–1914) was not born in the house around the corner on what's now called Holland Street. But he may have lived there as a young child."

Patrick pulled one of his historic books off the shelf, and pointed to a page documenting the fact that Holland's father worked for the Coastguard.

"So J.P. would have been born in their house in the barracks," Patrick concluded with a wink.

"Now, about the castle up the street?" I prodded.

"It hasn't been there very long," said Patrick. "Only since the 1700s. And Liscannor itself has not been in existence very long, either," he noted this as he showed me a rare, fantastic hand-colored map of Clare from John Speed's 1610 atlas. What is now Lahinch (An Leacht) was a small dot spelled Liskeny.

I said to Patrick, "I have always had a fascination with maps—perhaps because I was a cartographer in a former life."

Patrick didn't skip a beat, while we turned from the large colorful map, we progressed to some small engravings—book plates—and then I noticed a lovely landscape in oil.

Patrick, enjoying my curiosity said, "It was done by a woman painter in the 1930s."

"Absolutely charming," I beamed with delight.

As our conversation turned to art, I mentioned that I have been an art dealer for over thirty years. This prompted Patrick to tell me, "My first wife was from Oklahoma and was a painter of some note."

He then opened up a bit more and said, "I have a major collection of books at home—seven times the size of this shop!"

I was feeling like we were on the same wavelength when I asked, "Do you have any catalogue raisonnés?"

To my delight he said, "Yes, tons, Morris Louis, Ed Ruscha— and loads of books on architecture."

Ah—a kindred spirit. By now I was ready to buy everything in the shop, including the Taittinger bottles designed by Masson, Lichenstein and Rauschenberg plus the bottle of Cristal for €235!

Hmmm…champagne or playing the great links courses of Ireland? Alas, golf won out.

Note: The bronze sculpture outside the Cliffs of Moher Hotel (*page* 69) depicts J.P. Holland emerging from the first fully commissioned submarine of the U.S. Navy; it was called the *Holland VI*. The sculpture was designed by local County Clare sculptor Shane Gilmore (Dysart) and cast in the Connolly family foundry works in Kilbaha, Co. Clare.

MOY OR NO MOY

July 10, 2010

The other night while having our customary romantic dinner by candlelight—we now have a proper candle-holder with one 3″ wide × 4″ tall candle that melts inward, which replaces a rustic block of wood holding an "individu-ally foil-cupped Kinsale-Candle Night Light for Every Occasion," (in other words a wee tea light)—I looked over Kevin's shoulder (as he gives me "the view" to the bay), and I asked, "What is that big white building on the other side of the bay? Is it just one house?"

To which he replied, "That is Moy House."

We then talked about the fact that before he bought the lot our present house was built upon, Moy House was up for sale and he went to have a look with an idea to purchase it.

It was so run down, requiring many tens of thousands of Irish pounds, that he quickly abandoned the thought.

There it now stands, across the bay, registered in Ireland's *Blue Book of Irish Country Houses and Restaurants*. It is described as having a "sensitive restoration of an early 19th century estate, creating a contemporary and eclectic ambience...with eight oversized rooms on 15 acres and commanding hilltop views over Lahinch Bay, enhanced by mature woodland and the meandering River Moy." The book also says it has a "traditional Drawing Room and a Zen-feel lower Library area." Sounds lovely.

Too bad I am not at all confident about driving Kevin's car while he is away at Old Head—especially in the rain with the sort-of-intermittent wipers, or I'd go have a look.

Moy or no Moy really defines: is there a mist, a fog, or a downpour? Can I see Moy House or can I not? As the crow flies, it is probably only three miles away. Well, I *can* see it, but it *is* raining.

In fact, while it looked like it was not raining *yet*, I thought I would take a walk up to the gas station/shop to get some soup or something warm in time to watch The Scottish Open on TV over at Loch Lomond. I figured on bringing my good golf umbrella (a perfect souvenir from Turnberry) in case it started to rain on the way home.

As I got out the front door, it was, in fact, already raining. It was gentle enough with no real wind. That is, until I got around the corner. All hands on deck! Man the sails! Two hands on the tiller!

I made it to the store and back with a microwavable container of Erin Soupfulls Chicken & Country Vegetable soup, nearly soaked-through jeans and Moy House now disappeared in the mist.

But I know it is there—and someday, I promise myself I'll see it from the inside, while having a piping hot bowl of seafood chowder as I look back across the bay and see, or not see, our charming little white house on the water's edge.

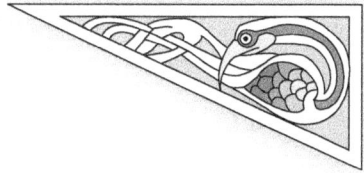

SOLID AS A ROCK

July 11, 2010

The fiercest wind of all visited us last night—well, visited me—alone here in the house. Kevin was still away playing golf with the lads—now in Waterville. Wind whistled into places I didn't know existed. This was *way* beyond blow-y which is windy, but that is mere wind.

The wind was gusting and the rain had already closed in when my friend Frances, who was down from Limerick, came to pick me up for our girl's dinner night out. It may have been the first time that nobody secretly snickered at me for wearing my cashmere Burberry "Happy Scarf." Frances took me to a place in Lahinch that I had not been to before called Kettler's Restaurant on—Kettle Street. Charming and cosy. I had a caesar salad starter and a delicious dish of salmon and hake.

For the compulsory side dish, I asked our server, "For green vegetable, what do you have?"

She answered, "Mixture of veg with broccoli…will that do?"

"Yes, that sounds fine, but please don't bring me any potatoes," (I have probably eaten several pounds of this Irish staple in the past month.)

I suppose I shouldn't have been surprised when the dish arrived with three billiard-ball size potatoes and a piece or two of broccoli. If only I had known there was such a thing as the steamed spinach, which arrived as a little dollop atop my main course, I would have asked for that and been in seventh heaven.

With the light lingering until past 10 PM, Frances was able to drop me at home and get back to her hilltop house in Lahinch, hopefully without any sloshed surfers or stumbling golfers who had gone for one too many pints, riding as a hood ornament on her SUV.

My first clue for what kind of blustery night I was in for was not being able to get the front door shut and locked. The strong, Atlantic wind whipped and whirled all night. It was a symphony of scary sounds. Was I ever glad to have an eiderdown comforter to keep me warm, as I could not snuggle with my far-away Stallion. I had to make do with my thick Old Head socks.

After reading a good chunk of my book, my eyes finally closed and sleep took over. I woke to a much calmer brightness. But there were telltale signs of how wild the wind was—especially in the entry, where the rug was blown about a foot away from the door and little pebbles and snail shells were strewn about the tile floor.

When Kevin called in the morning, I described the perilous night and told him that a lesser house may not still be standing! It is a comfort to know that ours, which sits by the rocky coastline of Liscannor Bay, is solid as a rock.

We've talked about knocking it down and building a real dream home, but it would probably take a few Sherman Tank Battalions just to get the roof off and the entire 1st Armored Division to level the rest!

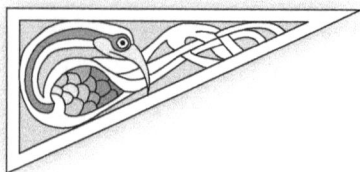

PLAY IT IN MY HEAD

July 12, 2010

I t was sunny enough yesterday morning and I was eager to get in a walk while the weather was mild. It has been raining on and off lately, mostly on, and I quickly grabbed my camera and donned a golf cap to shade my eyes, as I have temporarily (I hope) lost my sunglasses.

This was a perfect opportunity to walk along the Cliffs of Moher road and get a closer look at the ruin, which I have so far seen only from the car window. Just one problem—I needed to marshal my courage to get through one perilous stretch of road where even a pint-sized person like me has not an extra inch of walking space before being smack up against the massive tangle of prickly hedgerows.

For several days I have been considering what measure of mettle I would need to get through this treacherous quarter of a mile. In fact, the fear prompted me to search for our copy of the popular Tom Coyne book, *A Course Called Ireland,* to reread the part where he describes how the giant tour buses zooming by would brush the hair on his knuckles as he *walked* from course to course, circling the entire coast of Ireland.

I remembered this passage came early in the book, so I just started at the very beginning, which is hilarious anyway. And now that I *live* in Liscannor and have been playing mostly at Kevin's home course at Lahinch, having reached the part where he has gotten to the fourth of 56 courses that Coyne played—that being Lahinch—I can tell you that his Lahinch story is worth the price of the book!

What makes his story even more endearing is that I now know the course so well. Part of my recent rounds have been just walking with Kevin in his fourball, where I am often on their tees witnessing their massive drives, and, ahem, occasionally helping to find their balls in the dense dunes-y grasses.

It is like Loch Lomond for me, where they just played the final round of The Scottish Open yesterday. (Oh happy day—Darren Clarke claimed second on his own which qualifies him to play in the Open Championship later this week at St. Andrews—who says you never remember who comes in second?)

Although Loch Lomond is not a links course, it is one I truly love playing. It even pleases me to know that the tour players are playing the 16th as a par 4 but from the forward tees, we play it as a par 5. I have often relived the intoxicating moment when I made par there—which felt like a birdie to me.

So now that I have slipped into this pleasant reverie, I have subconsciously summoned the nerve to walk up to the ruin.

I even have the added benefit that although I am just around the shoreline from the dunes of Lahinch, when I am not able to be on the links, I can play it in my head. Better still, I can drive the ball 280 yards like Kevin, hit my 3-wood over the Klondyke to 5 feet, cut the ball into the wind, reach every par 5 in two, make every putt inside 20 feet and of course I never lose a ball.

No video simulator required!

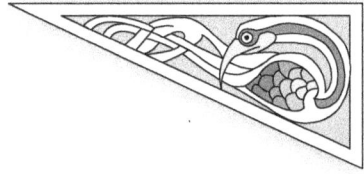

SEAHORSE SURPRISE

July 13, 2010

So what's the news like over here? There are the broad-sheets—two of the most respected newspapers are, "*The Irish Independent*" (being the broadest of broad and nearly unmanageable for my short arms) and *The Irish Times*. Then there are the more tabloid types.

When I dropped by McHugh's for a bowl of soup I had a choice of *The Irish Independent* and *The Star* or *The Daily Mail*.

"What's the difference between these papers?" I asked my server, when he brought the cutlery and the glass of wine I ordered.

"The *Star* and *Mail* are smutty," he answered, adding, "*The Irish Independent* is more truthful."

"Okay, thanks, give me the truth."

The news that is reported in the daily newspapers can range from a feel-good story like this:

> *A horse owner in Country Kildare is celebrating the birth of twin foals. Equine twin birth is so low—maybe 1 in 10,000,*

*and most often one or both are lost. The foal is named Lucky
and the little filly is Angel. The mare Molly is a six-year-old
thoroughbred—mated with a Clydesdale stallion.*

To the more tragic:

*After the World Cup matches, seven youths piled into a car
with only five seat belts, which went out of control on a wet,
windy road in Co. Donegal and then plowed head on into a
66-year-old man driving home from Bingo—leaving them all
dead—in the country's worst ever car crash.*

Pages and pages of stories on the economy, home values
heading further south, bank repossessions on the rise, are
sobering. Not much sympathy in *The Irish Independent* for
former Anglo Irish Bank chief Sean Fitzpatrick, who is
declared bankrupt and will "have to rely on his wife's
€3.6 million."

There is political wrangling all over, exemplified by a story
about the HSE (that is the Health Service Executive, which
provides health and social services to everyone in Ireland)
being "derelict in their duties" regarding safety of children
in foster care.

And then there is TV.

Back in the early 1970s, when I first landed in London at
the age of eighteen, I think there were all of two channels.
Now there is a dizzying array of channels, on Sky for
instance, ranging from Sports, Entertainment, News,
Lifestyle and Culture to a station devoted to Documentaries.

After watching a bit of CNN and BBC, I switched over to the documentary about seahorses and an entrepreneurial team hoping to be successful at commercially breeding them in captivity in the west of Ireland. Here's a fascinating and surprising fact: the female impregnates the male, who gives birth to a "cloud" of baby seahorses that are about the size of an eyelash.

Who knew? And if you buy one, there is one other sweet surprise—you even get a birth certificate!

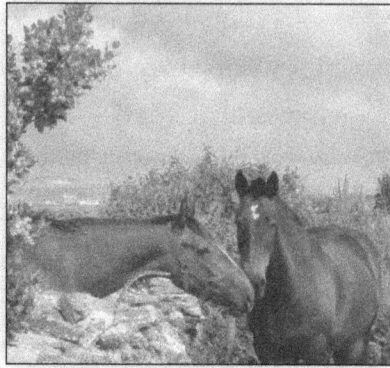

WAITING BY THE WALL

July 14, 2010

On and off throughout the day, I observe the horses in
the adjacent fields waiting for each other at the stone
wall. Inevitably the two in the east field are joined by the
three in the west field, but it is mainly the pinto and the
newish horse I call Star that interact the most.

What was at first nuzzling is now nipping and perhaps even
some biting. I haven't quite worked out which one is the
Alpha alpha male. I thought it was Pinto and today it looked
to be Star. Probably they are trying to work it out too.

I decided to do my own little experiment when I went for a
short walk at 8:30 PM—it is a "moisturish" evening but not
raining at the moment. Although I can't be in either field, I
am close while in our driveway just on the other side of the
east pasture that has a sort of fence—made of three flimsy

bands of white plastic tape, which I think carries an electrical charge. In fact, tonight I walked down to the corner where the field makes a turn and I could hear a distinct clicking noise.

As the three over there and the two over here were all just grazing on the grass in their fields, I am the one who stood near the wall just to wait and watch what would happen. My intention was that they would get used to me, just standing quietly, not moving, and then eventually accept me and ignore me.

In no time at all, Pinto seemed to feel me silently call him and he started to walk straight at me and came to the wall. As soon as he made his move, the other two horses in his "herd" followed him to the wall. Then, just as abruptly, Star and his companion strode over to the wall. And there we all were! As they were moving, I slowly took a step forward. And then another.

The convocation had officially come to order! As always, it is Pinto and Star who carry on with the rest of us being in attendance and mainly just watching with all our ears pitched forward. Display of dominance or grooming, I am still not sure, but there was definitely a bit more aggression with a neigh thrown in here and there.

Perhaps they know my smell now and no longer regard me as an intruder. Seems so, as we all drifted away from the wall, none of them stopped to stare at me in my grey pebbly pasture…just one of the herd.

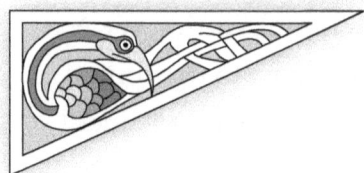

NOTTATALL

July 15, 2010

Whenever I hear someone say "not at all," in customary lilting Irish it sounds like, "Nottatall." It reminds me of a comical story that Kevin tells that goes like this:

"An American woman asked a local garda (policeman) in the town of Killarney what does the yellow line mean? 'It means you cannot park there attall (at all).' Then what does the double yellow line mean? 'You cannot park there attallatall.' "

Maybe this is one you don't get unless you hear it yourself. "Like you know?" That is another one you hear over here. Kevin used to say it so much, like you know, that I teased him, like you know, so that he would realize he said it a lot, like you know like you know? That cured him. Like you know.

Nottatall is endearing. Goes with: "It's no bother."

The other thing that is sweet to my ear is the charming patter of any common question or comment that might be:

"I thought you said you'll be coming down to Lahinch on Thursday—do you think you can make it by 5:30 so we can get in all eighteen holes?"

Which would sound like:

"I taught you said you'll be coming down to Lahinch on Tuuursday—do you tink you can make it by half five so we can get in all eighdeen holes?"

Once in a while when I have that hangdog look—that just about cracks Kevin up—he says, "Oh you poor ting (thing)" and then we both dissolve into a laughing fit. It has recently evolved in to, "Oh you poor tingamajig."

What time is it? "It's just gone two."

And we don't go over to the car mechanic when we drive over…"Let's call in to the mechanic."

Of course when we call somebody, we pick up the phone and call, right? No, we don't call Nigel, we *ring* Nigel.

Have you got all that? No? Will there be a quiz? Nottatall.

NOT TOO BULLISH
ON BOATS

July 16, 2010

Ominous clouds looming got me moving out the door, but the drops were already dropping. However, they stopped before I managed to put up my umbrella. Good. That meant I could walk down to the harbour and maybe find out just how far away is Moy House across the bay?

I came to the Cliffs of Moher Cruise ticket hut—the sign, a bright yellow affair—stuck onto a shack of sorts, where normally one or two guys sat in rickety chairs out front, usually smoking cigarettes. I didn't want to buy a ticket—I just wanted to know how far away is Moy House. In my goofy brain, I figured I would at least amuse them and say I was curious because I was thinking of swimming across.

But today it was a girl by herself at the ticket hut. I asked her, "Is the boat going out today?" It was very low tide and the harbour was just an icky smelling sea of mud.

"Yes," she said, "maybe in an hour and a half. The tide is coming in *very* slow."

She sounded so American, I just had to ask, "You're not Irish, where are you from?"

"Colorado…I'm just hanging out for the summer, visiting family over here."

"How nice is that?" I said with a smile to this adventurous kindred spirit, acknowledging our mutual good fortune to find our American selves on this side of the Atlantic Ocean.

It also turns out, when I asked her if she had any idea what was the distance, "as the crow flies," from Moy House to Liscannor, Kate (her named turned out to be) replied, "It's about five kilometers (about three miles) and a friend of mine actually decided to swim it!"

So there ya go! Goofy brains abound…and I got my answer!

Then, remembering that it was her job to sell tickets, she asked me, "So, do you want to buy a ticket?"

Hmmm…I'm waffling because it is such a little boat and it will feel even smaller if the sea gets choppy. Besides, I already got what I came for.

Appealing to my own curious nature, she revealed, "You can see secret things like a wild herd of goats!"

I was looking up at the sky trying to gauge if the clouds would open up. Better have a bowl of soup and come back.

Then I realized I did not even have the €20 ticket price and would have to walk home for more money. "Uh, Kate, I'll have to think about it—I might be back…"

I decided to reverse my course and walk toward the gas station shop to see where the Holiday Home road would take me.

Just before the gas station, I turn back toward the sea and noticed there is another road up to the right. Great. I found a back way to get to that interesting looking ruin I'd spotted while racing by in the car. And even more exciting, there was a field of cows! Aha, another chance to check them out, as yesterday, on the treacherous stretch along The Cliffs of Moher road, by complete surprise, I found myself just inches away from a huge Holstein. At least, I was pretty sure it was a Holstein because of its distinctive black and white coloring.

Although there was a nearly five-foot, brambly stone wall separating us, I had unknowingly entered her "flight space" (I learned this from the documentary about cows on TV the other night). She bolted and galloped away, all 1,500 massive pounds of her. What a sight. I am not sure who was more startled. I jumped myself, but an oncoming car was charging up the narrow road and pinned me back up against the thorny brambles.

As my heartbeat returned to normal, I came upon another field with a herd of grazing cows. Then came the sound of the bovine animal kingdom, the likes of which I have never heard. This was no moo. This was a whale of a wail. Having learned my lesson, I slowly crept up to the stone wall to discover the bull of bulls down in the corner, again, separated by a shoulder-high stone wall from the cows in the adjoining pasture.

Oh mercy! To think of the wild uproar he would cause if he could *bull*doze through that wall. I got one photo of the mud-flinging randy wailing giant and just then my camera battery went dead and the lens zipped shut.

No point on going on the boat ride today, as it would take a few hours to charge up the battery.

Too bad. The sea has never been calmer and the threatening clouds never opened up. Besides, I would rather take the boat out of Doolin which is four times bigger and probably has a loo!

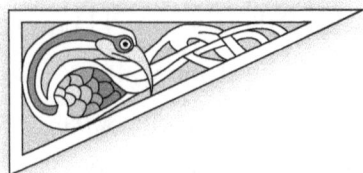

SPOT OF BOTHER

July 19, 2010

Just like in 2009, I enjoyed watching the final of The Open Championship on the Old Course in St. Andrews while in the same time zone—but nothing can compare to the excitement of the 59-year-old Tom Watson having a putt to win in '09 at Turnberry to tie Harry Vardon with six Open wins. Full of anticipation after our own intoxicating round at Castle Stuart in the Scottish highlands, we hoped to witness the fairytale unfold. Watson's miss from just off the green on the 18th was devastating. It was clear that he was deflated and our heartbreak was so huge, we could not even watch all four play-off holes with the ultimate winner, Stewart Cink.

When I saw the crowds on the Old Course at St. Andrews, it brought back fond memories of being there in person in 2005, with media credentials and some access to places regular ticket holders can't go. However, the greatest privilege of all was to watch the final round and to see the leaders hole out on 17, tee off on 18, and finish on the green of the "Tom Morris" hole, while I was holding a glass of champagne and viewing it all from "The End House," owned by Kevin's friends, Gordon and Shelagh Murray.

Now it is five years since Tiger's second win there—and although some held high hopes that he could summon the magic again, he was not a contender in the final round. Although another bright light, Lee Westwood chased (and eventually took second place), it was the South African, Louis Oosthuizen, who calmly plotted his way around the Old Course while playing with Paul Casey in the last pairing.

Oosthuizen was beyond surgical in dissecting the course. He was pure zen. There was hardly a note of high drama—especially after Casey found himself in a spot of bother taking a seven at the 12th hole. He steadied the ship, but the wind was existentially out of his sails. Could it be McIlroy's star rising? There was a chance that the golf gods could reward his heroic effort, as all the other lacklustre Irishmen slid down the leader board. In the end, it was the laudable Louis who would wear the label of Open Champion and hoist the Claret Jug with a staggering 16 under for a seven-stroke victory over Westwood.

After the forgone conclusion came about on the 18th hole and the new champion was crowned, we switched off the telly and turned our attention to our delightful house full of mad keen golfers.

I offered a toast to our guests and thanked them for coming to our happy home and said, "Having you here makes me feel so special and blessed," as I barely knew them with this being my first full summer in Liscannor.

Chef Kevin had made his gorgeous lamb and roasted vegetable meal, and we all tucked in with great relish. While the food was devoured and the wine flowed, P.J. Leyden (who is Irish but lives in England with his wife Una most of the year), kicked into a high humorous gear and had us all riding on a tidal wave of laughter while he regaled us with stories of "The Major," a blustery blowhard, whose contemptuous arrogance flowed in every direction.

But The Major was nearly apoplectic when it came to women on the golf course. Apparently he was a former British officer, and he pontificated his highbrow anti-suffragette view that went something like, "If women can't understand how Parliament works, how can they possibly total up a scorecard?" Women anywhere *near* a golf course was such an anathema to him that he would snort and steam and rail that, "They should all stay the hell away or be shipped off to New Zealand." Sort of an upper-crusty version of "women should stay barefoot and pregnant"... and in the kitchen of course.

Sean and Bernadette Scanlan, Dodi Hanley, Una, Frances, myself and Kevin were all doubled over in laughter enjoying the craic, especially after the story about how The Major, famous for his prodigious consumption of alcohol, was found asleep one morning in his car in a fairway bunker after an intoxicating Captain's Dinner at Lahinch.

Our festive feast was topped off with an exquisite Tiramisu, made by Frances. But beneath the joyous atmosphere, like the mist rolling in on the bay, was a quiet current of loss, with all of us knowing that we were missing two more merrymakers—David and Ailbe, who shared many spots of bother as two of Kevin's regular fourball at Lahinch—and who had gone to the "fairways in the sky" within the previous four months.

They would have made us a perfect and transcendent table of ten.

DAPPLED FRIENDS

July 21, 2010

Imagine my surprise when I walked out my front door to check on my horsey neighbors, only to discover a new little jumper in the field. Here was a youngish girl on the prettiest pony rounding a few fences, that just sprung up overnight.

Under the watchful eye of (most likely) her mother, the petite equestrienne negotiated the modest obstacles on her willing mount. I was fascinated by this new development in the otherwise peaceful pasture, and my research revealed that early horse shows, which included jumping, started in France, where the course spread out over the countryside.

Since this was not popular with spectators, fences were brought into an arena and the sport became known as "Lepping." Then in 1869 the "horse leaping" came to prominence in a Dublin Horse Show (now one of Ireland's largest events and a summer highlight). I had no idea that when I go to Dublin tomorrow I will be in the cradle of Irish Show Jumping!

I was eager to see who would be waiting at the wall the next day, and I was delighted to find the grey spotted pony alongside Star, who nearly eclipses the smaller horse when she swings her starboard side around. Star sees me first and saunters my way. Then the little spotted grey ambles over to have a look at who is joining the herd. It doesn't take long before they are both bored with me, for I haven't come with any treats.

They moved and munched their way around the corner in the L-shaped field, and I followed them with my camera. To get a better photo of the diminutive dappled grey horse—could it be a Connemara pony?—I climbed up on a stone wall, and lo!…found a gorgeous snail sitting serenely on the flagstone. Hello? Anyone in there? The wee critter is housed in a spotted—no, dappled—brown and black shell with lovely whorls. It is definitely not coming out to see if I have any treats.

I truly feel like I live in a world of wonder—a tiny creature here, a giant creature there, appearing magically in the landscape. With sheets of rain falling last night, and intermittently again today, I am curious—where have my dappled friends gone to?

They have all disappeared!

Thankfully, my own Stallion is right here beside me.

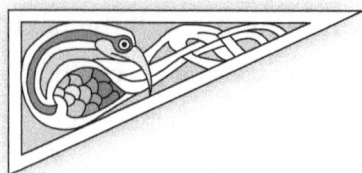

CHICKEN
UN-SUPREME

July 23, 2010

I'm looking forward to the drive to Dublin for numerous reasons, not the least of which is dinner at Wong's. You would find it hard to believe that a Chinese restaurant could be worth the three-and-a-half-hour drive, but I swear it is. The experience is more akin to dining in an elegant steak-house—Morton's comes to mind. Dark mahogany paneling, silk damask wall covering, sophisticated lighting, and white linen table clothes create a classy atmosphere. And no tacky fortune cookies—Belgian Chocolate to finish.

Now comes the food. We don't even bother with the extensive menu. Just order our favorites—Kevin's favorites—which suit me just fine. Lettuce wraps, with crunchy minced pork (no, P.F. Chang's didn't invent this starter, but it is our favorite when in the U.S.), perfect crispy duck with a steaming hot pile of delicate pancakes—always too many—the reverse of the American serving, and then something like sweet and sour chicken with vegetable fried rice, that is light as air.

Tonight will be dinner at Cruzzo's in the charming seaside village of Malahide. Sure to be sensational. Then tomorrow night after golf, a very special treat—dinner in The Joe Carr Room at Sutton Golf Club with a group of guys flying in from Florida by private jet. The gastronomic extravaganza topped off with a lunch at The K Club on Monday before returning home to Liscannor.

So you thought the food in Ireland is not all that good? Think again! On the southwest swing, when golfers stay and play at Old Head, they are not only experiencing one of the most spectacular golf courses on earth, they luxuriate in the Member's Suites and dine like royalty. I am sure they drink like Romans, since they don't have to drive anywhere—just negotiate the spiral stairway down to their suites.

Then it is on to Killarney, where they will play at Waterville and Tralee, and have at least one memorable meal at Nick's. Again, no menu required. Just bring on the Lobster Thermidor and let the good wine flow…and flow, until the rhubarb crumble arrives.

In fact, Kevin was travelling with some clients a couple of weeks ago on this itinerary, and the night he was dining on that lavish lobster meal, I was having something a lot more modest. I was only able to buy something within walking distance to our house in Liscannor—that meant finding something at the Top gas station/convenience store. At least this time I remembered to bring my own bag.

I picked something out of the frozen food case that looked, um, like it had not been there for the last five years. Yes, Chicken Supreme, *sounded* good too. But it turned out to be the gooiest, unsavoury mess. So much so, that I wound up eating Pringles and a slice of Romantica with a glass of wine, or rather whine.

So, moral of the story—hang with Kevin and you'll dine like a king!

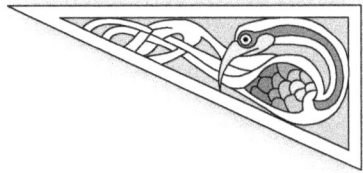

CANOES ON THE ROOF

July 25, 2010

The American lads were set up to play their match yesterday at Portmarnock Golf Club (founded 1894) at the leisurely hour of 2:30 PM, after the club competition was over. We arranged for Willie to pick us all up in his luxurious coach at 1 PM so we could have a bite to eat before going out on the course. I was looking forward to just walking along with Kevin's foursome as an observer—a most pleasant and nonstressful way to be on a golf course.

Jimbo, the "designated drinker" of this group that came in by private jet—would also be just walking along (and replenishing the adult beverages) for the other foursome. Four Irish versus four American. Me and Jimbo comprising the gallery of two!

It being Saturday, this was our only chance to take Kevin's watch back into Weir & Sons in Dublin, where it had been sent away to Patek Philippe to be fixed, but now it needed a minor adjustment. Thus we had just a few hours to make a quick trip into the city on the Kevin Express. With Kevin being a Dub, and having lived in the village of Portmarnock

(*Port Mearnóg*) for years, he flew us into town piloting our BMW jet-on-wheels. Even when not in a hurry, Kevin only knows two speeds—fast and faster!

We left the charming town of Malahide (*Mullach Íde*), and sped through the towering trees and high hedges, passing by the ancient walls encircling Malahide Castle.

Like a movie in fast forward, we zoomed through one little town after another, passing the wee Artane Cottages—the size of a two-car garage in America—that is, as long as the cars were no bigger than an Opel Corsa or a VW Golf. We zipped by Apache Pizza (*Apache Pizza?*) in Donnycarney, flew past Marino where Kevin's mother and grandmother lived long ago, dashed by the footballers in Fairview Park where even in the clingy rain, the dog walkers were out in abundance for their morning stroll.

We slowed slightly as we approached a red light…willing it to turn green, and then it was back to barrelling along, one fish & chips, burger, kebab place after another. And then, wait a minute. Did I see what I thought I saw? It looked like a pile of canoes on a little flat roof. And in a flash, they were far behind us. Nah, couldn't be.

Suddenly we were dwarfed by the giant double-decker Dublin buses, as having left the sleepy suburbs we slipped over an imaginary line into the city.

Yikes! We were heading straight for the massive, modern green glass AIB Building. It felt like we've crashed right into a Roy Lichtenstein painting. Whaam! The Ulster Bank looms large by the River Liffey. Whoosh! The impressive Custom House dominates the other side. Left. Right. Park. Mad dash to Grafton Street—the premier shopping district—that thankfully has been pedestrianized.

We sprinted over to the multi-story, landmark building that is Weir & Sons (the premier jeweller of Ireland, founded 1869) to see about Kevin's watch. We entered through the handsome front doors into the rarified atmosphere of the elegant store full of diamonds, gold, silverware and china.

No time to wait for an elevator, we bounded up the stairs two at a time, passed the gorgeous leather goods, steered around the Mont Blanc pens, charging through the gift departments full of fabulous Faberge and beautiful Bulgari and hurried over to the Customer Service Department.

"Ah, Mr. McGrath, what brings you back so soon?" wonders the gentleman who took care of sending Kevin's watch to Switzerland for service.

"I tried twisting the stem to wind it and it just fell completely off."

Obviously used to handling many fine timepieces, the gentleman tried unsuccessfully to rejoin the stem to the case, but it just wouldn't cooperate. Back to Switzerland it goes.

"It's not going to take another four months to get it back again, is it? " Kevin hints after waiting so long.

"I'll put a rush on this for you Mr. McGrath," the gentleman smiled accomodatingly. "I'll ring you as soon as it's back."

We go at a furious pace, dodging the throngs of shoppers, Saturday street performers, students, and tourists outside Trinity College, darting through the dense inner city traffic, zig-zagging around the Hop-on Hop-off Dublin Bus Tour drivers, jumping into our gutsy BMW, strapping on our seat belts to fly back out the Malahide Road.

(There should be a little bubble here, like the comic-book style pop art painter was known for, where it says: "No wonder Lichtenstein was commissioned to paint a Group 5 Racing Version BMW car!")

Now in fast reverse, we were charging once again past the park, the pizza place, the fishchipburgerkebab shop, and then—for a fleeting moment—Yes! A huge pile of canoes on a roof. I'm not crazy, they are canoes!

SHAMPOO

July 27, 2010

Monday found us at The K Club—world famous for hosting The Ryder Cup in 2006. We rejoined the group of golfers from Florida (known as the Sunshine State) who were keen for a rematch with the four golfers from Ireland (sometimes known as the Moonshine State because of its prolific distilling of *Poitín*, pronounced "potcheen," an illegal, highly alcoholic beverage made from malted barley grain or potatoes).

This jovial group of American guys, who seemingly existed on an intoxicating all-liquid diet, were once again accompanied by Jimbo, their fun-loving drinking buddy who I previously named the "designated drinker" (the DD).

Arnold Palmer (*b.* 1929), winner of seven Major Championships, 62 PGA Tour events, and 95 professional tournaments during his long playing career, brings his exceptional experience to golf architecture and now includes dozens of courses all over the world in his portfolio, including the two courses at The K Club.

Our lads played the Smurfit course on Sunday, stayed overnight in the lavish resort, and we were down for the match on The Palmer Course. Two foursomes. Four Irish versus four Americans once again like the other day.

Cloudy with "sunny spells," enough wind to make things interesting, Americans have caddies, Irish players/K Club members do not. I'm walking with Kevin's group again, while the DD accompanies the other foursome like at Portmarnock on Saturday.

The parkland courses and the luxurious resort all have a five-star-plus feel. Purchased by The Jefferson Smurfit Group in 1988, and opened as a resort in 1991, the property comprises 550 acres on the former grounds of the Straffan Estate in County Kildare (thus the "K" in K Club). Straddling the River Liffey, it is the complete contrast to most of the links clubs/courses built 100+ years ago.

Even the "visitors" locker rooms are quite luxurious— the Members Only locker rooms accessed by coded card. Corridors display floor-to-ceiling photographs of all the players, drama and dignitaries on hand for the 2006 Ryder Cup.

Result of our own match: All square. OK...now let the drinking begin. The DD wants to know, will I have a glass of champagne? *Oh yes please!* And when that one evaporates, would I like another glass of shampoo? *Oh yes please!* You get it. Dicky bird is a word and shampoo is champagne!

The tipsy lads are jetting down to Old Head this evening for a round of golf there tomorrow before flying into Shannon for luxury coach transfer down to Doonbeg on the west coast of Clare.

We wave goodbye to them as they board the coach (the fully stocked bar on wheels) taking them back to their private jet waiting at Dublin airport…and then Kevin asks me, "Would you like to have a look inside the hotel?"

"Indeed I would!"

From the Versailles-like chandeliers to the hand-carved marble mantles, I revelled at being inside these sumptuous surroundings. Marvel after marvel after marvel. First, a monumental Botero, then an entire room full of Jack B. Yeats paintings; and last, an incredibly gorgeous and elaborately illustrated tome on a table-top stand (with a discreet "Do Not Touch" sign). It just took my breath away. Then I realized there was an equally incredible slip case with rich Celtic decorative designs. Grandest marvel of all: gold embossed lettering on the spine: *The Book of Kells.*

Now that I've seen the surrogate, I'm really excited to behold the famous illuminated manuscript at Trinity College. Good thing the National Treasure is housed just around the corner from Temple Bar…where I am sure to find a glass or two of shampoo!

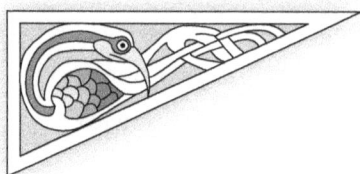

A RARE BREED

July 29, 2010

I can't believe it took me this long to figure out that I have actually seen an owl. About two weeks ago, while I was doing some stretches on the floor, I happened to glance out the window and see a most remarkable, brightly colored, large bird, sitting on the stone wall.

I'm in a hurry, but trying to move slowly so as not to create any disturbance (would I even be noticed 25 feet away inside the house?), I pointed the telescope on this gorgeous creature, hoping it would stay put. Mind you, floor-to-ceiling windows wrap around three sides of the living room facing the bay, which is why I could see this awesome animal while my head was on the floor.

Twisting this way, twisting that way—wow—I have never seen such a thing! A completely new creature has suddenly appeared in the panoramic picture of field, rocks, water and clouds.

Absolutely marvellous. And a mystery to me until I realized that with such gigantic eyes and a minute beak, it had to be an owl. Then it occurred to me, I have never seen an owl in my entire life! Yes, I have *heard* one, but never *seen* one.

So as not to forget its shape and coloring, I made a primitive sketch of the bird's profile with a large, round head and equally round body, and my notes say:

Eye as big as beek! (I wrote it that way in my haste.)

Arrow pointing to small beak: grey.

Arrow pointing to body: copper and black.

My research of Irish Owls revealed that I had sighted a short-eared owl, or *Asio Flammeus*. And if that isn't exotic enough, the Irish name is *Ulchabhán réisc*. As the word flammeus suggests, the feathers looked like flames.

All I can tell you is, seeing this owl was a magical experience. I truly felt transformed while it was in my vision. There is no explaining this heightened vibrational sensation other than to say even though the short-eared owl is diurnal (active by day), they are a rare breed, and for it to appear to me was phenomenal.

I felt extraordinarily special for the privilege of getting to see this rare and magestical bird. Now how often can you say that in the course of any given day?

THE ISLAND

August 3, 2010

Sandwiched in-between hosting our guests at
Portmarnock and The K Club, Kevin and I managed
to get out to play The Island on the Sunday, July 25th.
It was a bit unfortunate that our only possible time to play
there fell on the day of the Ladies Member competition,
so we went out at 12:40 PM, the first available tee time after
the final fourball.

We were so warmly received by David Costigan, the Head
Professional in the golf shop, and greeted so graciously on
the first tee by Dónal O'Meara, the Captain, and Council
Member Miriam Hand, who took our photograph. We were
setting off on our adventure feeling very special indeed.

I had heard about The Island Golf Club some years ago, and
was eager to finally have a chance to see this classic links
course for myself. From James Finnegan's *Emerald Fairways
and Foam Flecked Seas* to Tom Coyne's, *A Course Called
Ireland*, it has been highly revered. I must say, it exceeded
my expectations.

Kevin hits a very long ball, so we let the ladies clear the first green before teeing it up. I had a good shot up the middle. Uphill par 5, then a downhill par 4 and a rollicking roller coaster the rest of the way. Blind shots, doglegs, greens tucked behind dunes…even a long par 3 reminiscent of the blind par 3 "Dell" at Lahinch.

Now that I live in Scottsdale, Arizona, I found it particularly amusing to find the 5th hole named "Desert"—this hole was the blindest of blind. Quirky like Machrihanish.

It felt like the whole concept of elevated tees originated here, as the heights and the views over the dunes and to the sea were intoxicating.

By the time we got to the 14th, the course had slowed considerably with the competition still on. It would have to be our last hole. At least I could finish with what may have been the best drive of the day onto the narrowest five-yards-wide fairway, with water all the way up the right side and a towering dune running the length of the hole on the left. Intimidating.

Fourteen is a shortish par 4 named "Old Clubhouse." I had plenty of time while waiting to note the bronze plaque set into the side of the tee box reading: "Steps and Foundation of the Old Club House are Part of This Tee." It also tells the story of how the golfers came by boat to The Island from its founding in 1890 until 1973. There is even a small boat full of golfers depicted in the bas relief.

Kevin said, "Do you know, I remember coming by boat myself the first time I played here!"

The signal to the boatman to collect the golfers was a large red and white disk which was hinged in the center and could be seen from the shore.

Time got away from us and we needed to get all the way to Blackrock for an early dinner with Kevin's daughter and family. Hopefully we'll be back again some day to finish the final four holes—and perhaps next time, to help with the blind shots, we'll bring along a seeing-eye dog.

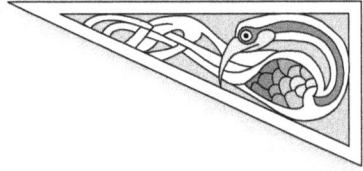

HELLO SKIN

August 6, 2010

We set off on our way to Limerick (*Luimneach*) at the invitation of Sean and Bernadette Scanlan, to play golf with them at Castletroy. To my amazement, Kevin had not played there before. They are also members of Lahinch and have a second home not far from us in Liscannor.

We actually arrived a bit early, having our virginal experience going through the brand new tunnel under the River Shannon. Big. Clean. Nice. And behind us that fast.

With the club being just a few minutes away, Bernadette let us unload our clothes at their lovely home, called The Cedars, before going on to Castletroy Golf Club for our virginal adventure on the golf course. C'mon, how many times in your life can you say you are a virgin?

This is a long parkland course—playing even longer due to it being so wet. Founded in 1937, it is both beautiful and mature, with views of mountains in the distance like the "Keeper." Bernadette was pleased with her stableford points, as she was planning to play in Lahinch in the Lady Captain's Prize over the coming weekend. What do they call those horses that just help the thoroughbred keep up his time for the race coming up? I wasn't keeping score so much as keeping pace, enjoying the track.

Laura, one of the three Scanlan daughters, joined us for a fabulous meal at a trendy new restaurant in downtown Limerick called Chocolat. We got on the subject of words and phrases and how odd things sound to the unfamiliar ear. She told us how one of her co-workers would greet her with "Hello Skin."

"Oh. Is it cheeky?" I wondered.

"No, not at all," Laura explained, "It is a sweet way of implying that you are friends—close friends—close like your own skin."

I had told Laura I've been writing some stories, and when we got back to The Cedars, she gave me a book, *The Return Journey* by Maeve Binchy. I adore it. Don't want it to end. It is a collection of short stories. She and Bernadette were shocked that I had not heard of the very famous Maeve Binchy before. Now I know there are another 18 of her books I must read before I die.

Like my introduction to Seamus Heaney's poetry through one of Kevin's Irish friends living in the States, I am that much more overjoyed to have this book put into my hands by someone here in Ireland. Like tasting a delicious food for the first time, the *virginal* experience is all that more memorable. I know, I am overdoing this virgin thing.

As I am a book lover, I was absolutely over the moon about yet another book I happened to notice on a table near the kitchen by floral artist Reverend Mac: *Beyond Mere Words*. A floral artist herself, this is Bernadette's passion.

Staggeringly gorgeous, eccentric floral designs coupled with world-class photography, the likes I had never seen before.

I was truly blown away, but I promise not to use the V word.

EMPTY FIELDS

August 8, 2010

I'm sad. All the cows are gone. The field has been empty for days. I miss them terribly. And to make matters worse, Paint is gone and so are the other two horses on the west side of the stone wall. Now where have *they* gone?

Shortly after the little grey pony arrived in the east field, the other three horses disappeared. And then the cows. Just like that. At first I thought they could be someplace in the large field where I couldn't see them. But no. My bovine neighbors are really all gone. They are not up on the hill by the castle ruin where I could check on them with the tele- scope. They are really really gone.

Now the dappled grey pony, I will call Connemara, because I think she could be a Connemara pony, is very quiet. Good temperament. Good disposition, I suppose the breed- ers would say? She is dominated by the larger horse in that field. But it used to be Star and now Star is gone too.

For a few days, that field appeared to be completely empty— perhaps during the time of the Dublin Horse Show. Could they be trailered away? Even to Dublin?

I read that some believe the Connemara pony developed from Scandinavian ponies that the Vikings first brought to Ireland. Did the Vikings borrow my pony?

Another legend says that when galleons from the Spanish Armada ran aground in 1588, the Andalusians were set loose. Has the Armada been resurrected and my dappled friend been captured?

The entire romping, chomping herd of cows are…where? Not in greener pastures.

Although I have that empty feeling when we've been abandoned, I hope all my four-legged friends will one day come back, as there are no greener pastures than here by the water's edge of Liscannor Bay.

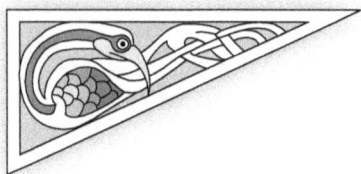

PARTAKE

August 9, 2010

It was a wet and blustery day. "Will we play?" Frances, my Irish partner, asked by text. "Yes we will," was the decision taken by the foursome. I was delighted that Frances asked me to play in the Ladies Invitational Fourball at Lahinch on the Castle Course about a week ago. But I wasn't so sure now because of the weather.

Unfortunately I struggled in the wind and the rain and wasn't much help to my partner. In spite of my poor play, I enjoyed the experience immensely, for the simple reason that it was my first round in an authentic Irish Ladies event. We were paired with another member, Helena, and her guest from the east side of Co. Clare.

On our way to the second tee was when I think I learned there was a "little money" on the game! Small amount—bets on 6, 6, and 6 (six-hole matches). Frances kept track of all this, which wasn't too hard, as we were mostly down.

What made it especially fun, though, was the banter. Helena, who plays off about 7, had a plucky sense of humor to match her strong game. So when I asked her, "Is any putt given? What if it is just six inches?"

"Well it depends. In a friendly match? Yes, unless somebody is being particularly bolshoi," (Irish for pigheaded) was her jocular answer.

On the back nine, we found ourselves doing a lot of waiting in the fairway because Helena could reach the par 5s in two. There was an exceptionally long wait on the par-3 thirteenth, as we were obligated to hold up an extra few minutes until the group before us cleared the 14th tee before hitting our tee shots.

We had time for an entire conversation about competitive golf and golfing for the fun of it. Helena relayed a story about some young players lamenting their poor performance. And that is when she said, "It is really too bad when people get so caught up in winning, that they forgot what it feels like to just partake."

In a single word, she had summed up what I have been wanting to articulate about *playing* golf. Partake. To partake. It seems all too often, in America, but not so much in Ireland, that there is hardly a bit of playful banter. So much more emphasis is on performance.

Add to the banter, we are walking. Walking and talking. And playing golf. It feels so much more natural. The pace and rhythm are ideal. As fast or faster than shuttling around in a cart.

In fact, one day I mentioned to Bernadette while we were at Castletroy, "Some courses in the U.S. don't allow you to walk."

"You're joking me," she said, utterly shocked.

And no wonder. It is shocking and sad that so often in America, golfers have lost (or never had) the sense of joy that comes from playing golf, where partaking is the rule, rather than the exception.

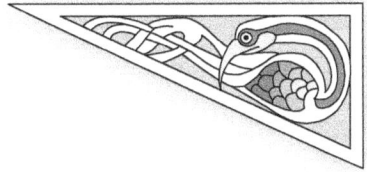

COUNTRY OF CONTRASTS

August 10, 2010

A Dublin-based Irish friend said to me recently, "Here in Ireland, there is the well-looked-after and the run down." In small towns like Ennistymon, they are often side-by-side. Take for instance the crumbling cottage on the corner of Ennis Road and the nearby charmingly painted pub on Main Street called Eugene's that calls you inside whether or not you are craving a pint or a seafood chowder.

You certainly expect grandness from the former estates like the Straffan House, forming the heart of The K Club, or the aristocratic Adare Manor—that are now 5-Star hotels or exclusive private clubs.

But I was recently bowled over when a friend of Kevin's asked him to come take a look at a private house when we were down in Killarney last Friday. We're not sure why— perhaps she thought we could use it for special clients on a very high-end golf trip—so we made the effort. The visit was sandwiched in between a meeting with the Deputy

Mayor of Killarney and playing golf at Tralee—a stunning links course designed by Arnold Palmer (and God, "who surely designed the back nine," says Palmer)—at the gateway to the Dingle Peninsula.

We were off to see the house—somewhere near Dooks—another course I am eager to play some day. After numerous zigs and zags on tiny unmarked roads, causing Kevin to nearly blow a gasket, we finally arrived at "the house." The grounds of the 14-acre estate were absolutely magnificent, with views of a secluded lake, meticulously manicured walled gardens, and stately groves of towering trees.

The original house had massive additions expanding in every direction. From the extremely formal dining room to the much more modern kitchen, the house exuded taste and sophistication. Some of the artwork suggested a passion for horses—racing in particular. The cavernous wine cellar was stacked to the rafters. A carriage house had been made into separate guest quarters—with a clever light-filled loft.

It was a world unto itself. Totally transforming. We emerged back into the verdant countryside, racing down this road— nope, wrong way—spin around, go the other way, trapped for awhile by a "dangerous" tree, being cut down, to finally get on the right road to Tralee. We had to call to push back our tee time, which I was not unhappy about in the least— as the gap allowed the extraordinary opportunity to savour and appreciate a true well-looked-after hidden gem of the highest magnitude.

A WHITER
SHADE OF GREEN

August 14, 2010

Just as you come over the narrow stone bridge from Lahinch toward Liscannor, sits a minty green house at the bend in the road. It is the color of pistachio ice cream. With a tasteful stone wing on the right side and a horse trailer in the driveway, it is a most attractive sight.

In a country known for its forty shades of green, this would not be one of them. It is more like a color you would find in South Beach or maybe Portofino. The magnificent spectrum of Irish green would include gorse bush green, ivy green, yellow green, hedge green, blue-green, beech tree green, evergreen, marram-fescue-bent-Yorkshire-fog-sedge and meadow grass green, you know what I mean green.

There are the occasional surprises—usually a shop or little café—pink here or lavender there. And sometimes you see the rich, salmon-y color like The Black Oak Restaurant, which is thankfully not black.

Another popular color is yellow—could be a house or a pub. Probably another forty shades of yellow over here: pastel yellow, dirty yellow, mustard yellow, pale yellow, blue-trimmed yellow, beige-y yellow.

Don't get me wrong. All the green is a constant source of delight.

Why just today I discovered a lost Rothko painting out my dining room window. From the ground up it reads: Big band of grass green, slither of stone grey, generous band of silky smooth blue grey, patchwork pasture green and a giant mass of cloudy grey.

That is until the Cliffs of Moher boat comes along—creating a new streak of white across my Rothko. And just as fast as it shows up, it dissolves away again. Artful magic.

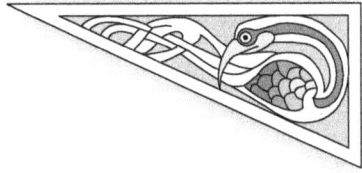

CHECKPOINT

August 18, 2010

We were heading up to Lough Erne (*Loch Éirne,* meaning "Lake of the Érnai") for a meeting at the resort and to play a round of golf on the gorgeous parkland course before Kevin's practice round at Donegal (*Dún na nGall*) the following day. Coming out of Ennistymon, we took the zig-zaggy route over the mountain that brings us by the village of Carron.

Mile after twisty mile, we traversed through The Burren (*Boireann*), a magical limestone landscape rich with historical and archaeological sites. We came to the pass that cuts through the massive rock mounds, and at last the windy bumpy road brought us over the crest of the last giant hill. The clouds parted, the drums rolled, trumpets blared and there was glorious Galway Bay—made famous by numerous Irish folk songs and beautiful enough to inspire John Lennon and countless other modern musicians.

A large group of golfers coming over in October—on the recommendation of a local Irish videographer—have been booked into Markree Castle, just south of Sligo, so we decided to have a look at it. We rarely use properties we are unfamiliar with, but this was one time we made an exception. In the heart of Yeats country, the castle has a very colorful history dating back to the 17th century with the invasion of Ireland by Cromwell.

Their official history reads: The young officer, Edward Cooper, was serving under Cromwell when his army defeated the mighty O'Brien Clan. O'Brien himself lost his life in this battle and Edward married his widow Máire Rúa (Red Mary). She had her two sons take the name of Cooper as protection from the English invaders. Cromwell's army marched on, farther northwards in spite of the fact that he did not have the means to pay his officers. Instead, he gave them large pieces of land. Thus, he gave Markree Castle and the surrounding grounds to Edward Cooper. Until then, Markree had been a fortified outpost of the McDonagh Clan. It is now a renovated (but *cold*) stately setting for many a wedding, with a stunning stained glass window in the hall.

After passing through Leitrim (*Liatroma*), the smallest county in Ireland, it was onwards to Lough Erne, which meant crossing into Northern Ireland. No more signs in Irish (Gaelic), and fences fences fences. No more tidy stone walls. They are big into barbed wire here. It was the same grey clouds and showery forecast, but somehow the clouds felt heavier and the grey was greyer.

Once in the gates of Lough Erne, you are in another world. Turreted and castle-like but thoroughly modern and luxurious. Kevin and I totally enjoyed the golf course when we played it last September and we were looking forward to getting out there again. The tenth hole would be my favorite. Just as I holed my putt for par, a magical rainbow appeared, as if to say, "Well done Taba!"

After another enjoyable round, we had a quick bite to eat in the grill at the clubhouse, and the journey to Donegal resumed. We were zipping along at the usual fast clip on the undulating loughside road when we were flagged over to STOP.

The RUC (Royal Uster Constabulery) officers were all dressed in black with bulletproof jackets and machine guns. *Machine guns!* I have not seen such a sight since flying into Manchester in the mid 1990s during "the troubles" with the IRA.

"Let's see your driver's license," one gruff officer said to Kevin as he put down his window. "What's your hurry?"

"No hurry really," Kevin said calmly.

"Why did you overtake that car just ahead of you?" demanded a second fierce-looking officer.

"I thought he was slowing down and was turning in to the left."

"Where are you going?"

"I'm heading up to Donegal to play in the Ulster Seniors Golf Championship."

"Oh, so you're a golfer are you?"

"Yes, we just played golf at Lough Erne."

"What did you shoot?"

"I shot in the mid 70s"

"Okay, on your way, hit 'em straight."

This encounter was sobering to say the least, and we thanked our lucky stars that apparently one of the machine-gun-wielding military officers must have been a golfer. We hadn't heard of any conflicts in the area, but we certainly drove along at a gentler pace for the twenty minutes it took us to pass through Belleek and cross the border into Ballyshannon.

Aaah. We could breath a little easier, back in the land of good "craic," where the next checkpoint would be at our hotel, and all they would be looking for was our credit card.

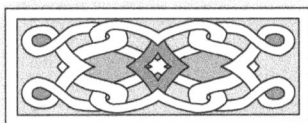

MURVAGH

August 19, 2010

We arrived in Donegal very late on Tuesday night so
Kevin could play a practice round at Donegal Golf
Club on Wednesday morning. His idea of a "holiday" is
playing in the Ulster Seniors, which started today. When
the ominous morning came, I went out at 10:04 AM with
him and another competitor from Dun Laoire, but came in
to the clubhouse at the turn. The play was painfully slow
and when the menacing clouds down poured for the third
time, I sought shelter. It was certainly a day when you
could experience all four seasons in your backswing.

Along with a bite to eat, I availed myself of the small
booklet in the golf shop commemorating the 50th
anniversary of Murvagh (1959–2009) as it is often referred
to by the locals—and have now increased my golf geekiness
by a significant margin. I learned that when Eddie Hackett
(1910–1996) was commissioned in 1973 to lay out this
course on a 180-acre tract, for the modest fee of £200,
he cleverly used Muirfield as a model, with the front
nine running counter-clockwise around the perimeter

of the peninsula, and the back nine forming an inner clock-wise loop.

Hackett, ever modest himself, was known to say: "I found that nature is the best architect, I just dress up what the Good Lord provides."

It was the highly esteemed Pat Ruddy who was hired in the mid 1990s to make some changes over the next few years, and we did see him arrive yesterday to play in the tournament as well. I had actually discovered, a couple of days before while reading in the *Official Golf Guide* for 2010, published by the Irish Tourist Board, that some redesign at Enniscrone was taken on by the "late Pat Ruddy," so we had a good laugh when the "late" Pat Ruddy arrived in his customary good humor.

If it were not for the unfavorable conditions, I might never have learned that the Irish Hare is Ireland's fastest mammal and they live in nests called "forms." And did you know that the badger is Ireland's largest carnivore? They live in underground tunnel systems called "setts," The starter on the first tee warned us of a pesky resident badger who had been tearing up turf, and sure enough we saw evidence of his nocturnal activity on the 16th tee.

Perhaps the keen horticulturist and common golfer alike will be amused to know that included in the fifty species of wildflowers found here on the seaside links at Murvagh are: Sneeze Wort, Dog Violet, Common Vetch, Devil's Bit

Scabious, Yellow Rattle and Bladder Campion. I am sure they are all prettier than they sound.

But the most interesting species of all is the bag-carrying-or-trolley-pushing-ball-chasing-two-legged-golf-obsessed mammal who will travel great distances all over the world to play the most challenging game known to man. Both Kevin and one other playing partner—a delightful man who lives in Cork and is the author of the charming book *Lazy Days at Lahinch*—today carded 79, missing a few putts by inches, to rob them each of a more magical number. Tony lamented, "I had a score by the tail."

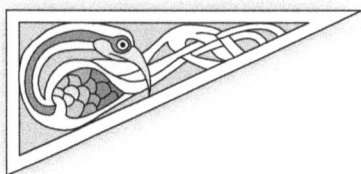

LOTTERY ON
THE GREENS

August 20, 2010

We're at the final of the Ulster Seniors at Donegal and it's blowing a gale. Then the rain shows up. Harsh conditions to say the least.

Kevin's foursome, including Tony again, tees off and there is trouble from the very first shot. Out of bounds for one. Lost ball for another. We go on to the second hole named Westward Ho, the tee box being to our right off the green, so we have switched direction into the teeth of the gale force winds. It is ranked the most difficult hole on the course, and it lives up to its reputation.

The third, usually the easiest of the par 3s, was not easy at all. In fact, it was another disaster. The 4th could be a birdie hole on a calm day, but the drain cutting through the fairway and the deep rough provided extra trouble today. More frustration.

Now we've come to the fifth, known as The Valley of Tears.

The name says it all. Off the tee you must carry all the way to the narrow elevated green. Anything short disappears into a huge hole. Left or over is a steep hill full of knee-high rough. Right is just plain lost. That's us. We just lost Tony who has run out of balls.

The Long Ridge, the 6th hole, changes directions again. It is longer and more ferocious than ever. The 7th hole makes another turn, basically heading back toward the clubhouse. Hole 8, Moyne Hill, is another par 5 with a blind second shot. More tragedy takes a third player, leaving Kevin and just one other golfer to complete the round.

I gave up too and sought refuge in the warm, dry clubhouse. It was more than a couple of hours later when I finally saw Kevin and his fellow competitor slogging up the 18th.

We waited around for all the groups to get in and learned that nearly a third of the field didn't even finish! Some were "WD" or Withdrawn and other were "NR" meaning they couldn't finish for one reason or another so they did Not Return their scorecards. In fact there were so many NRs on the big old-fashioned leader board, that they had to use WDs instead because they ran out of the little plastic letters!

Kevin made the supreme effort to finish, shooting 50 on the front and miraculously 39 on the back for a total finishing round score of 89, fourteen strokes above his average.

Tony, either NR or WD, when he finally appeared in the clubhouse, to commiserate with the many wounded warriors, confessed that he was so demoralized, and in particular, it was such a "lottery on the greens." However there was one winner of the lottery today and that was Garth McGimpsey, former British Amateur Champion and Walker Cup player, so probably the best man won after all, no lottery ticket required.

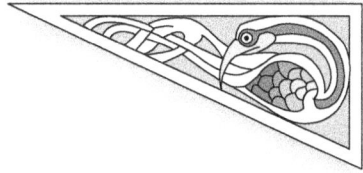

KISS ON THE LIFT

August 22, 2010

etting underway to Rosslare (*Ros Láir*) on Sunday morning really started the night before when we learned about the road closure out of Liscannor to Lahinch for a 17,000-person bike ride event. This meant moving our departure up to 8 AM to get through the blockades.

Thankfully we zipped along the quiet roads and put our-selves on the other side of Tipperary (*Tiobraid Árann*) fairly fast. We passed by a sea of cows—they looked like miniature Holsteins—almost dainty, compared to the Clare cows, then zoomed through Kilkenny (*Cill Chainnigh*) with the profusion of yellow and black flags flying in anticipation of the All-Ireland Hurling Final.

As we approached Waterford (from Old Norse: *Veorafjoror/ Vedraford* meaning "ram fjord" or "windy fjord" and Irish: *Port Láirge* meaning "Larag's port") around noon, the temperature had climbed to a tropical 20 degrees (68 Fahrenheit). We were impressed by the massive campus of the Waterford Institute of Technology on the River Suir, and wended our way through the historic part of town to the newly opened House of Waterford Crystal.

The entire experience calls to mind one of my favourite Oscar Wilde quotes: "I have the simplest tastes—I am always satisfied with the best." The Sporting Trophy Replicas and the Statement Pieces on exhibit were proof positive that Waterford has risen from the ashes of its tragic furnace closure to resume its centuries old legacy, proudly presented in the Park Avenue-like lavish retail store. From the polished marble floors to the giant chandeliers and all the sparkling crystal on display, we were duly dazzled.

Our jaunt took us through Enniscorthy (*Inis Córthaidh*), with stand after stand of mouth-watering strawberries around every bend. Now it was on to Bunclody Golf & Fishing Club, in Co. Wexford. We arrived just in time for a bite to eat in the brand-spanking-new mostly glass clubhouse, topped off with a surprisingly cool-looking thatched roof!

Under mostly sunny skies, we set out on this two-year-old parkland course, weaving its way on the grounds of the former Hall-Dare estate. Designed by Jeff Howes and stretching to over 7000 yards, it is full of good, testing holes. And yes—there were people fishing on the River Slaney on the back nine.

We finally reached the piece-de-resistance—the elevator that takes you to the 18th hole. It is as it sounds—unbelievable! Nestled into a heavily wooded area behind the long

136

par-3 seventeenth, we climbed a steep hill to the tall tower rising another six stories.

Surrounded by dense trees on three sides, Kevin and I squeezed ourselves with our golf bags into the glass-enclosed lift. The temptation was too much when we were skin to skin in the cramped space.

"Kevin, this is so romantic. Kiss me. Kiss me." After fifty more feet of stolen kisses, we emerged a bit giddy and stumbled out of the steamy little box.

In his elevated state, (oh forgive me this) Kevin produced the most prodigious drive on the downhill, dogleg right par 5. Hitting a heroic shot with his fairway driver to fifteen feet and setting up an eagle, my semi-pro Stallion missed the putt, but made birdie and won the euro!

We were both so intoxicated with happiness we felt like we could skip the ferry and take to the air ourselves. What a perfect lift-off for our upcoming journey to Holland.

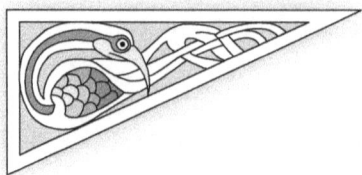

FERRY TALE

August 23, 2010

Following behind two metallic burgundy fully-decked-out matching Honda motorcycles (with trailers!), we drove on to the 9 AM Rosslare ferry to Fishguard, and departed the dock on time. We were comfy with WiFi and two Pullman chairs on deck 7 of the Stena Line. With endless cloudy skies, a west wind and a calm sea, we are sailing to Wales, where along the way to Holland, we will begin our quest to play three more of the Top 100 courses in the world—starting with Royal Porthcawl.

Our main reason for embarking on this 10-day journey to Holland is to celebrate Kevin's sister Gerri's 60th birthday. All of Kevin's siblings will be coming from all over the world, like they did for his 60th birthday last year in Liscannor on the Emerald Isle.

Walton Heath and Porthcawl will merit stories of their own, but perhaps the most looked-forward-to round of all is Morfontaine, #54 on the Top 100 in The World (2009, *Golf Magazine*). North of Paris in the Chantilly, Oise region, I am told it is tougher to get on than Augusta.

We are guests of Laure de Gramont, the granddaughter of the aristocratic owner.

In 1913, the 12th Duc de Gramont (1879–1962), a keen golfer, engaged the eccentric Englishman, Tom Simpson (1877–1964) to design a nine-hole course, near his estate Chateau de Valliere, on what was originally a polo field. In 1927, Armand de Gramont once more commissioned Simpson—whose clients included Royal Lytham, Cruden Bay and Ballybunion—to design an 18-hole course. With some recent alterations by the American architect Kyle Phillips, it lived up to its reputation of being a "museum piece."

We have permission to invite some friends, so we are delighted that Nancy & Michael Bamforth, who live in Belgium, will be joining us. Nancy was born in France and Michael was born in England, however we are extremely grateful that they speak perfect French, as Michael learned from the Secretary-Manager when providing their handicaps, that the men are required to wear long pants. Thankfully we have been spared the embarrassment of Kevin showing up in his perennial favourite shorts. *Mon dieu!* That is, when we finally do show up—as our "route-planner" directions only bring us to the ancient town, and we are now looking for a place that does not want to be found!

Now on the tiny twisty roads of rural France, we finally came upon a elderly round-shouldered man ambling along with a walking stick. Kevin put his window down and asked, "Club Morfontaine?"

After taking a few seconds to size us up, the gentleman responded, "Go zis way to zee leetle bridge and zen you take zee road to zee right. You'll see zee gate."

We sped along at a furious pace, (normal by French standards) and at last found this oh-so-private place. A delicious lunch on the veranda of the ivy-covered, understated clubhouse—with a glass of wine (*bien sur!*)—and the four of us set out on our round. Other than one member playing by himself, we were the only people on the course. We started on the first tee near the sandy parking lot, and wove our way through the magical forest along the pine tree root-bound paths and lengthy heathery carries.

There is no way to describe this experience other than to employ another Oscar Wilde quote: "The true mystery of the world is the visible, not the invisible."

With a little rain and a lot of humidity, we completed our round, full of wonder and a very good appetite for a fabulous meal in the medieval village of Senlis. *Saw-lease*. Nancy taught me how to pronounce it correctly.

We parked near the magnificent cathedral (dating to the 12th century) and in the fading daylight, negotiated the ancient cobblestone streets to Porte Bellon, where Nancy and Michael had stayed and eaten the night before.

"Something to drink Madam?"

"*Oui, s'il vous plait*, I'll have a glass of shampoo!"

What else could a champagne-loving golf geek do?

A true fairytale day.

CELTIC CLASH

August 24, 2010

We alighted from the ferry in Fishguard and were welcomed with some sunshine. We're back to miles instead of kilometers, but boggled by spelling that only the Welsh can decipher. No longer in the Emerald Isle—land of forty shades of green—we are now in Wales with only 39 shades of green and one other distinct difference—the roads are much smoother.

We must ARAFWCH NAWR as we have a WYNEB DROS DRO due to TREFN FFYRDO O'CH BLEAN because the FFORDOO AR GAU.

Which is to say that we must reduce speed now as we have a temporary road surface due to a new road layout because the road is closed ahead. Or something like that.

While we are stuck behind a truck, listening to a CD, all of a sudden in a *booming* voice, BBC Radio overrides our music with a traffic report at a deafening decibel level "...lanes blocked, still queuing on the road to Swansea although the accident is long gone," the voice tells us. Okay! After inching along, we finally start moving.

We hadn't been in Wales for more than a half hour before I realized we were seeing 10 times the number of BMWs that we might see in a single day in Ireland. Zoooom. There goes the first Porche Carrera since leaving Scottsdale—opening the throttle between the speed cameras. As our movie unfolds, the contrast piles up—there's a guy in a red T-shirt beside the road having a pee while a sleek black Bentley slithers by. Clash of low class and high class.

No way we'll make our tee time at Royal Porthcawl. "Not a problem," they say over Kevin's cell phone, "we'll get you out when you arrive."

The weather has taken a dramatic turn for the ferocious and we were now about to tee off in gale force wind. I could barely stand much less get my ball on the tee…and keep it there! Daunting. At the 12th hole, the rain came down like angry fists. I gave up trying to play "extreme" golf, and made my way back over the heaving hills full of gorse and broom to the clubhouse, where I could behold the rugged sea and absorb the history of Porthcawl from the confines of the cozy bar.

Founded in 1891 on a nearby piece of land, the original nine holes were laid out by Charles Gibson, the professional at Westward Ho! The present layout was extensively modified by the esteemed H.S. Colt in 1913, with major alterations done by Tom Simpson in 1933. This course has crept (back) into the Top 100 in the world, occupying place #100

(2009, *Golf Magazine*). I was impressed to read the actual letter dated 30 March 1909 from Herbert John Gladstone to Sidney Robinson, M.P. (1854–1930)—at the time the Vice President of the Club, which says:

> *"I am glad to inform you after inquiry and consideration,*
> *I have felt able to recommend the King to permit the club to*
> *use the title 'Royal', and that His Majesty has been pleased*
> *to approve the recommendation."*

While Kevin continued on to battle the elements, I soothed myself with a glass of Sauvignon Blanc, and had time to consider the clash between being inside the oh-so-refined royally ordained golf haven, as opposed to the raw, heaving, golf-ball-gobbling landscape outside—wishing I had more "ballast" so I could finish one of the great golf experiences of Wales.

Perhaps the golf gods will let me have another go on a calmer day.

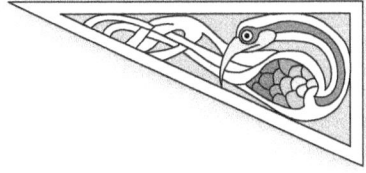

COME SEE
SOME GROUSE!

Morning, August 25, 2010

N ever was I happier to *not* play a round of golf that I had so much looked forward to... All the way from Celtic Manor to Walton Heath, Kevin and I slogged through persistent rain. We pulled in next to a Corniche and sat in the car park while deciding our strategy for getting one of our golf umbrellas out of the boot.

We arrived at this storied club to play #82 on the Top 100 courses (2009, *Golf Magazine*) well ahead of our 2 PM tee time, which became tea time. Or rather, we opted for a glass of wine and bite to eat in the bar, after conferring with the professional, Simon Peaford, over in the golf shop.

We discussed the idea of coming back to play the following Monday, which gave me plenty of time to marvel that this personable young man was following in the footsteps of James Braid (1870–1950), winner of the Open Championship five times and their professional for 46 years.

Ho! What good fortune. We settled in a cozy corner near the bar, where an irresistible book entitled *Heather and Heaven, Walton Heath Golf Club 1903–2003* by Phil Pilley was discreetly displayed. I was completely absorbed from the first few paragraphs of the Introduction where Pilley confesses: "The title of this book, by the way, is shamelessly plagiarised—though with consent from *The Daily Telegraph* of August 5, 2002. That day, Bill Meredith, reporting the English Amateur Championship, wrote that:

> "A bewildering burst of back-to-back eagles followed by a birdie lifted Richard Finch into a field of dreams at Walton Heath, a wonderful mixture of heaven and heather."

I merely changed the order of billing to ingratiate myself with the heather.

It only got better from here. A trio of members were passing through the bar and one stopped to chat with us—perhaps because he learned of our passion to play the highly revered parkland course.

"Hello, I'm Simon Creagh Chapman, the Chairman of the Green Committee, mind if I sit with you?"

"Oh please do!" Kevin and I said in stereo.

I drew Simon's attention to a quote by Bernard Darwin, one of my heroes, who said: "If there's something golfers want and do not get at Walton Heath, I do not know what it can be."

Simon disappeared for an instant and returned saying, "Here, this is for you!" when he graciously presented me with a pristine copy of the centenary history book to keep.

I gushed, "Thank you so much, for me, this is like back-to-back eagles!"

The whole magical encounter took another fantastic turn when Simon invited us into the inner sanctum of the clubhouse. There hung a magnificent life-size portrait of the champion James Braid, by Sir James Gunn, RA, *c.*1925.

On the way back to the bar, Simon pointed out another of the crown jewels—a Gunn portrait of the architect of Walton Heath, Herbert Fowler, who was an accomplished amateur golfer when he was commissioned to design the course in 1902.

Back at our table, Simon continued to astound us with stories of how his great grandfather was instrumental in founding Ballybunion in the 1890s. Apparently it all started with an invitation to "Come see some grouse!"

Once back in our car, after sliding my precious book out from under my rain-drenched jacket, I cooed to Kevin, "Sweetheart, aren't we lucky not to play golf here today!"

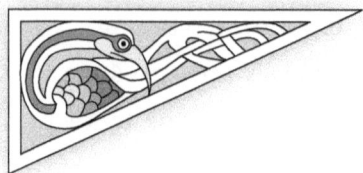

ANOTHER UPLIFTING
EXPERIENCE

Evening, August 25, 2010

K evin is a happy chappy because Tottenham Hotspur, a
soccer team in the English Premier League, are on the
telly. I am happy because I have a tub. Only half a roll of
toilet paper, but the tub is the key component. I ask,
"Sweetheart, how in the world did you become such a fan
of this team?"

He replied, "I've been following since I was a nipper."
Which explains nothing.

We are spending one night in Folkestone so we can get on
the Channel Tunnel early in the morning. Lashing rain. We
opt to leave the car in the coveted garage space and eat here
in the hotel. The Britannia is built to look like a cruise ship
but feels more like a down-in-the-tooth nursing home. Lots
of aged people hobbling around with canes and walkers.

The White Cliffs of Dover were outside our window in the
distance but were barely visible. We were enveloped in

persistent rain and fog, the magnificent sight was only in our imagination. When we called the front desk to inquire about eating in the restaurant, we were told it is for tour buses only. Oh geez.

We were dreading having to dig our umbrellas out of the car and trudge into the grey, wet town. Oh how glad we were to discover there was another restaurant where we could eat. Buffet only. That'll do. We're starving!

When we came down from the 7th floor, the lift was already jam packed, having gone up instead of down. It proceeded to stop on 6, where two jolly gigantic women insisted, "No worries, we can squeeze on!" And squeeze they did.

When the doors refused to close, we all chimed in unison, "You have to get off!"

With the elevator shaking and creaking, they waddled out as undaintily as they'd clambered in. Down we go to the next floor and this time a man and a woman tried to enter.

"You can't come on! The doors won't close!" we all said in chorus.

We were one big laughing bunch as we bounced the rest of the way to the lobby.

Our jovial mood disappeared the instant we saw the depressing room that held the buffet. The walls were covered in a dingy gold-flocked fleur-de-lis wallpaper and the lopsided ceiling fixtures made it feel like we were listing at sea.

We were ushered across a sticky wood floor and shown to a tiny table with mismatched, scarred chairs.

The mushy mess resembling Brussel sprouts looked like they were cooked in a different epoch. Having practically lost my appetite, I spooned some roast beef and carrots on my plate, but barely touched them, nibbling at a serving of mystery cake, and washed it down with a glass of sickening-sweet white wine.

I asked Kevin, "Are we going to look like those people?" shifting my eyes to indicate the table full of geriatric tourists over his right shoulder.

"I hope so!" teased Kevin.

It gave us a good laugh before squeezing back onto the elevator to retire to our room.

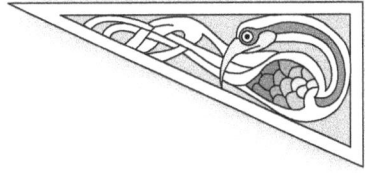

LOOKED GOOD
IN THE AIR

September 6, 2010

Golf in Ireland is highly entertaining. If you hang out with the Irish, your golf vocabulary will increase by yards.

It is great fun to walk with Kevin whenever he is playing in a friendly fourball—like the one at Lahinch recently. Handicaps announced, teams formed, the match determined and now it was time to hit away. Kevin teed up his ball and the fun began with Enda, a longtime golfing friend, claiming that Kevin is a notorious honor-stealer! After the banter and laughter, it is Enda who drives off first—with the lads chiming in, "Super strike," and Enda diplomatically claiming, "Lots of room in front of my ball," which is the Irish way of saying, "Let's see if you can hit it past me!"

We have plenty of holes where there is an encouraging, "Good recovery from there," or "That was one of the all-time great fours."

When we reached the blind sixth hole, a twosome competing in the semi-final of a juniors tournament played through—on their sixth play-off hole! When it was time for Kevin's group to resume their match, the line off the tee was, "Anywhere between those lads will be plenty good."

And no—we didn't hit into them, just joked about it.

One of my favorites is: "It looked good in the air." And if you are cheeky enough—you might say it to describe a bouncing putt. Now what you most often hear is, "*She* looked good in the air."

And why is a golf ball a she? I don't know. It just is. Like a boat, I suppose.

That particular day, we were all staring skywards and wondering, "Is the rain coming in?" After surveying the sky, Kevin the optimist quipped, "It might go around us."

It looked more and more ominous, and I decided to walk in from the 9th hole, knowing I could make it back to the clubhouse in five or so minutes depending on whether anyone was teeing off on the 18th or the 5th, or approach shots were flying over the Klondyke to reach the 4th green.

Since it stayed dry, I decided to walk into Lahinch town and wandered in to a bookstore. There I found a charming miniature book of Oscar Wilde quotes. It made me wish that Wilde had been a golfer—oh the rich quotes we would have—it would increase our golf vocabulary by miles.

He might have said, "Golf is like measles, should be caught young." But it is actually P.G. Wodehouse who said that.

Another likely Wilde candidate could be, "Golf is a day spent in a round of strenuous idleness." Nope, that's William Wordsworth.

Or how about, "Golf is so popular simply because it is the best game in the world at which to be bad." Sounds Wilde-esque enough, but that was A.A. Milne, creator of Winnie-the-Pooh.

Some say, "In golf as in life, it is the follow through that makes the difference," is a Wilde quote.

So who coined the phrase, "Golf's not a matter of life and death, it's much more important."

Why don't we just attribute it to Wilde? After all, he did say, "Life is far too important a thing to ever talk seriously about."

Which means it probably is Oscar Wilde who came up with, "She looked good in the air."

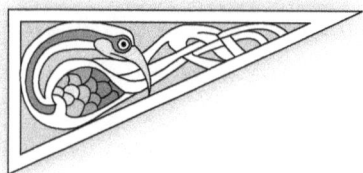

PINS AND NEEDLES

September 11, 2010

I really never knew anybody who is a sleepwalker, that is, until I met Kevin. It was a good six months before we made the discovery; and it was a big surprise to him as much to me!

In fact, we were visiting a friend in Florida in April a year ago, when Kevin got up in the middle of the night, to go to the loo, or so I thought. He wound up pulling the TV out of the armoire and nearly dropping it on the floor. The near crash and commotion was caused by (and also softened by) his open suitcase on the floor just in front of this tall cabinet housing the heavy TV.

Befuddled and buck naked, he then tried to get it back onto the shelf, behind the doors, but luckily I persuaded him to leave it where it was and monkey around with it in the morning. When he woke up, he did not have a clue what had happened that night and was mystified how the TV got inside his suitcase!

We laughed ourselves silly, and never told our host—but if he ever reads this, he will know who he is.

The most recent incident occurred just the other night, when Kevin howled like he had been stabbed.

"Kevin, Kevin, what's wrong?"

"Pins and needles."

"Where?"

"My arm."

"Which arm?"

"My left."

Then he got up, went to the loo, and came back to bed, only to scream bloody murder again!

"Kevin, Kevin, now what's wrong?"

"My *mumble mumble* hurts."

"What hurts?"

"My *mumble*."

That's when I realized, he was not even awake.

But I was wide awake…for about three more hours!

And sure enough, he had no recollection of it when I told him about it in the morning. Instead, he gets all giggly when I described his screaming, mumbling, and bumbling about. Then of course we have to relive the TV incident all over again, which always causes uproarious laughter.

If you yourself are a sleepwalker, or live with someone who is, you no doubt have some hilariously funny stories to tell. I am sure I will have more.

All I can say is, thank goodness Kevin hasn't figured out how to get the new flatscreen TV off the wall!

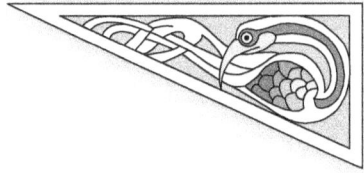

FOGGED IN

September 13, 2010

From dawn to dusk there has been no horizon all day. White caps and wind. And rain. Incessant rain. Kevin has said more than once: "It's miserable." Luckily we both have plenty of work to do, so being indoors is not a bother; but I confess, I have counted out the days (35) until we head back to the U.S.

There is no doubt that I am craving the warmth and the sunshine of Arizona. Being able to walk outside with shorts and sandals, any time, day or night, sounds very appealing right about now.

Don't think I wasn't noticing the bright green blades of grass glistening in the breeze the other day. And the rocks are even *hairier* since I first arrived. The hydrangea are starting to brown. There are still a few enormous and luxuriously big balls of pink and blue here and there, but they are fading fast.

The horses and cows are long gone. The busy bumble bees are absent. Most of the holiday homes are very quiet—

"Out of Bounds" and all the rest—very few cars around, even on the weekends now.

The surfers are still out there though. And yesterday while we played a very l-o-n-g round of golf on Lahinch, there were lots of colorful kites and parasailors riding the wind, while dozens of people strolled on the beach.

Nightfall is descending. From the upstairs window a few faint amber streetlights of Lahinch town are barely visible in the gloaming. It is the sound of the wind, blowing and bending itself around every hard corner, looking for a way in to any vent or tiny crack, that is pervasive. Wanting to be invasive.

The Atlantic is announcing itself in no uncertain way.

"I'm here. I'm always here. Even when I am calm, shimmering and hypnotic.

Then watch me stir myself into a frenzy.

You are small and fragile. I am mighty and forever.

Don't worry. I won't let you leave without showing you my sunny, gentle side. You'll miss me.

You already do."

FIVE STAR FUN

September 30, 2010

The "All Roads Lead to Doonbeg" Pre-Ryder Cup golf tour started out in a most elegant and dignified way. Several people came in early—some played golf at Portmarnock and others took advantage of a day of sightseeing in Dublin. With lovely sunshine, we had a grand tour of the city on the Hop-On-Hop-Off double-decker bus, which stops at 24 of the most visited tourist sites.

You would expect the highlight to be *The Book of Kells*, the ninth century manuscript, at Trinity College (founded in 1592)—it is certainly extraordinary. It is housed in the Old Library, as is the Brian Boru harp—one of only three surviving medieval Gaelic harps, and a national symbol of Ireland.

When we got to the Guinness Storehouse, the entire bus emptied out. After the short orientation, where we learned that the visionary Arthur Guinness (1725–1803) leased the original 40 acres for 9,000 years for a mere £45 annual rent, we could then ascend to the Gravity Bar on the top floor, to enjoy a "perfect pint" with 360-degree views of the city.

Not only was this the most authentic "black stuff," the bartender created the image of a shamrock on the creamy head that rises to the top, so each pint is a little work of art.

The following day, we assembled ourselves at the exquisite five-star Dromoland Castle, and conspired with our guest from Canada, Jim Larmond's wife Bonnie, to have all fourteen of us in a private room for a surprise birthday party for her husband. Was he ever surprised! Champagne (Shampoo) flowed, delicious food followed, and for the birthday boy and several others who stayed up late, the jokes and laughter continued into the wee hours of the morning.

We covered a lot of ground in the Southwest of Ireland—playing two rounds at the spectacular Old Head and staying in the five-star Member's Suites, then enjoying more golf at Ballybunion and Waterville with more gorgeous weather.

We then moved on to our last destination, the fabulous five-star Doonbeg Lodge, with a great many of us in the oceanview suites overlooking the 18th hole. Pure Heaven. With a 36-hole tournament, comprising rounds at Lahinch and Doonbeg, we congregated in the luxurious Long Room for our superb Gala Dinner, where the exquisite Tipperary Crystal trophies were presented.

After hearty congratulations to all the winners, Mick Begley, our Dublin-born entertainer extraordinaire, picked up his guitar and musically guided us all into the Irish tradition of a singsong. His vast repertoire that night included ballads such as "Fields of Athenry," favorites like,

"The Wild Rover," and a rousing rendition of the drinking song, "Dirty Old Town."

Then there was an interlude for the otherwise reserved Brandon Tise, from North Carolina, to take over the microphone, and he rocked the room with tunes like Don McLean's "American Pie" and Neil Young's "Heart of Gold."

Next, the Standers from Paradise Valley, Arizona, entertained us with a precious poem describing their whole Irish experience, before Mick resumed his seat and carried on with more Irish rock, pop and soul songs like Van Morrison's "Brown Eyed Girl."

And last, from the corner of the room, another friend from Dublin, Pat Duignan, singing a capella, brought tears to our eyes, with the popular folk song, "Red is the Rose."

After a long day of golf, prizes, a marvelous meal and great entertainment, most of us streamed out of the room and made our way to our exquisitely-appointed suites, full of original art and antiques, too tired to start up a roaring fireplace, and just fell ecstatically into our sumptuous beds, with pure Egyptian cotton sheets, mountains of plush pillows and Premium White Goose Down down-filled duvets.

Only to learn the next day that the party carried on—with the birthday boy—ending up shirtless in the bar after being provoked by the last few liquored-up hotel guests who asked him, "Hey dude, why are you wearing that sissy-looking shirt?"

So Jim says, "Here, have it, it will look better on you," and whips it off over his head.

Next thing ya know, everyone else whipped off their shirts! So there they were—*all* of them—shirtless in the bar.

In case you're wondering what to pack for your next trip to Ireland, you might want to leave the Hawaiian shirts at home!

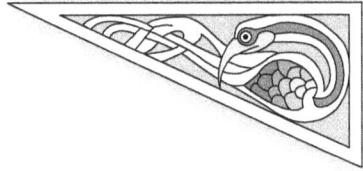

DREAMCATCHER

October 15, 2010

The first time I saw the "Here Comes The Bin Man" truck, I didn't know that everyone in Ireland doesn't have their trash picked up like we do at home in Scottsdale, Arizona. Why no, we have to haul our big black plastic bags to the Waste Management place and pay 4 euro per bag to dump them!

And then one day a bizarre looking truck came racing by us called "Let It Rain." Ha! It certainly rained on his parade when a few miles down the road we saw he was pulled over by the Garda for speeding.

Did you know there is a popcorn machine on the ice cream truck? Who knew popcorn was that pop-u-lar in Ireland?

Another surprise greeted me one morning when I poked my head out of the window while staying at The Grand Hotel in Malahide—a good size lorry announcing "Nosebag Fine Foods." Somehow those words don't seem to go together. Even though the truck sported a charming painting of a horsey animal with a canvas bag fastened around its head, it just doesn't have the right ring.

Somewhere else on the truck it said: "Eurofrigo." Probably just means it is refrigerated. But when you say it out loud, it comes out *You're a frigo*. How dare you call me a frigo! Take that back!

Strange trucks are all around—another was parked just outside the SuperValu grocery store in Ennistymon with gorgeous graphics for a company called "Dreamcatcher." Tastefully spray-painted on were the words "Film & Video Production." I'd hire them in a heart beat if I needed to make a movie!

Actually, I do need to make a movie…of this book. Look for *A Summer in Ireland*, coming soon to a movie theater near you!

LIFE IS GOOD

October 16, 2010

The row of twinkling lights in Lahinch town have diminished to just a few. Somewhere behind the hill the sun is rising, but today it is obscured by a thick mist which is quietly rolling in off the Atlantic.

Oh wait! Here comes a pink band across the crest of the hill. A reward for my patience. It is reaching upward. Intensifying. But just as fast—being overtaken by the mist.

Yesterday the sunrise was so dazzling, I needed to keep leaning to the left in my chair to keep from being blinded by the light. Either that or go get my sunglasses!

In two days time we will leave our lovely seaside home, so I am saying my goodbye, as we will go before the dawn.

Jaysus! Here it is powering up. The sun is looming. A brilliant halo is pushing higher. Higher. Pink to Orange.

A gentle band of blue appears above. Are the dense grey clouds breaking up? A white portal opens to the heavens above. Houses and rooftops materialize across the bay.

The silhouette of sea grasses are completely calm.

Just when I thought—just when I hoped the sun would burst above the hill—the fiery halo is gone.

It is the grey that dominates. But not in my heart.

As the symphony builds to a crescendo in the sky, now it is the water waking up.

Ripples along the shoreline will soon reveal the rocks below.

The tide comes in. The tide goes out.

Life is good. Life is good.

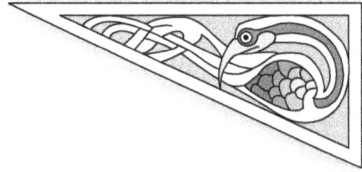

DOUBLE RAINBOW

October 17, 2010

Can there be any better ending to a magical summer in Ireland than to see not just a rainbow—but a *double rainbow*? Stretching from one side of Liscannor Bay to— OMIGOD—it is nearly touching down on our very house! It *is* touching down on our very house!

Oh, just the sight of it makes your heart skip a beat. Not to mention running out the door with the camera—to this side, to that side, into the grassy yard, backing up trying to get all of the outrageously gorgeous rainbows in the viewer while they are so effervescent. I'm breathless.

Why, it brings on the story of the mouse and the giraffe! If you're laughing, you know the story. If you are not laughing, you need to come to Ireland and Kevin will tell it to you. Life-altering experience. You will laugh yourself silly. Come on. You know you want to come over here.

Will you see a rainbow? Yes you will. Will you see a double rainbow? Ummmm. Not sure. But you will see many wondrous things. Ancient stone walls. Remnants of earlier

Celtic culture. Forty million shades of green. Animals. Forty million animals large and small. Big bulls. Countless cows. Thoroughbred stallions—you know who you are! Polka dot sheep. Goats. Hares. Pheasant. *Pheasant, you ask?* Bumblebees. Snails. Tinier snails.

And what will you hear? The sound of music. Everywhere. And song. The Irish have a centuries-old tradition of music and song. You will be energized. Your hands and feet will move. You will sing. You will cry.

The sea. Waves lapping on the shore. Waves crashing on the shore. Whether you love links golf (those of you who have not ever played golf on pure links courses *do love it,* you just don't know it yet) or just find yourself going for a walk on the beach—any beach—the ocean is your constant companion.

You will taste some of the best food you have ever "et." After all—this *is* an island nation—with abundant and delicious seafood. You will pick up the language, the slang, the idioms. You'll enjoy the craic. Don't know what that is? Come to Ireland. You'll find out.

What else did I find out in Ireland? After all the excitement of the double rainbow, while Kevin and I were sharing a glass of wine, gazing at the links of Lahinch out our dining room window, I mentioned that I used to want my ashes to be spread over Old Head, but now I think Lahinch. And what did my soulmate say? "Why don't you be buried here, beside me?"

So the double rainbow closes Chapter One and at the same time reveals Chapter Forty. Where I found a true and everlasting love—with a man and his country.

About the Author

Taba Dale has been a fine art dealer for 33 years. She cultivated her early love for all things beautiful through her frequent visits to the many world-class museums in Washington D.C. where she grew up. She took her first trip to Europe when she was 18, visiting thirteen countries over six months, thus igniting a passion for travel.

In the late 1980s, Taba moved to Avenel, a golf course community in Bethesda, Maryland. While jogging on the cart paths in the morning with the dew and at dusk with the deer, she vowed to take up the game some day. But first she created her golf company, Scottsdale Collection, specializing in publishing and selling golf art. It wasn't until twelve years later that she took a golf lesson, and after launching one ball off the sweet spot, she was hooked. Years passed before she could begin to actually play the game and live her dream after moving to Scottsdale, Arizona.

Curiosity about the history, tradition, beauty and the mystery of golf has led Taba to read the great authors, and study the renowned historians and architects of the game. She is now considered a bona fide golf geek herself.

Taba spends her summers in Ireland with her soulmate and life partner, Kevin McGrath, in their home near Lahinch in County Clare, where all three passions—art, golf, and travel have now converged to become the inspiration for this book.